AN INQUIRY INTO

The Human Prospect

Robert L. Heilbroner

AN INQUIRY INTO

The Human Prospect

W · W · NORTON & COMPANY · INC ·

NEW YORK

Library of Congress Cataloging in Publication Data
Heilbroner, Robert L
  An inquiry into the human prospect.

  Includes bibliographical references.
    1. Civilization, Modern—1950–   2. Regression
(Civilization)   I. Title.
CB428.H44   901.94′6   73–21879
ISBN 0–393–05514–0
ISBN 0–393–09274–7 (pbk.)

Published simultaneously in Canada
by George J. McLeod Limited, Toronto
PRINTED IN THE UNITED STATES OF AMERICA

6 7 8 9 0

FOR JOAN

Contents

ONE

Initial Reflections on the Human Prospect

THERE IS A question in the air, more sensed than seen, like the invisible approach of a distant storm, a question that I would hesitate to ask aloud did I not believe it existed unvoiced in the minds of many: "Is there hope for man?"

In another era such a question might have raised thoughts of man's ultimate salvation or damnation. But today the brooding doubts that it arouses have to do with life on earth, now, and in the relatively few generations that constitute the limit of our capacity to imagine the future. For the question asks whether we can imagine that future other than as a continuation of the darkness, cruelty, and disorder of the past; worse, whether we do not foresee in the human prospect a deterioration of things, even an impending catastrophe of fearful dimensions.

That such a question is in the air, hovering in the background of our minds, is a proposition that I shall not defend by citing bits of evidence from books, articles, and the like. I will rest my case on the

reader's own response, gambling that my initial assertion does not generate in him or her the incredulity I
should feel were I to open a book whose first
statement was that the prevailing mood of our times
was one of widely shared optimism. Thus I shall simply start by assuming that the reader shares with me an
awareness of an oppressive anticipation of the future.
The nature of the evidence on which this state of mind
ultimately rests will be the subject of our next chapter.
But the state of mind itself must be looked into before
we can proceed to an examination of the evidence, for
our initial perspective enters into and colors the
assessment we make of the "objective" data. Let us
therefore open our inquiry into the human prospect by
taking stock of our current anxiety.

As we shall see, evidences of this anxiety are to
be found in many advanced nations. Here, however, I
shall focus at first on the American mood, not only
because I know it best but because it has been itself a
bellwether of feelings elsewhere. If we then look into
the American state of mind, I think we can find three
main sources, or perhaps three levels of explanation,
for the pall that has fallen over our spirits.

The first of these I will call *topical*, to refer to a
barrage of confidence-shaking events that have filled
us with a sense of unease and foreboding during the
past decade or so. No doubt foremost among these
events has been the experience of the Vietnam war, an
experience that has undermined every aspect of Amer-

14

ican life—our belief in our invincible power, our trust in our government, our estimate of our private level of morality. But the Vietnam war was only one among many such confidence-shaking events. The explosion of violence in street crime, race riots, bombings, bizarre airplane hijackings, shocking assassinations has made a mockery of the television image of middle-class American gentility and brought home with terrible impact the recognition of a barbarism hidden behind the superficial amenities of life.

Perhaps even more important among these topical causes for our pessimistic frame of mind has been yet another development of the recent past—the failure of the present middle-aged generation to pass its values along to its children. The ubiquitous use of drugs, the extreme sexual relaxation, the defiantly unconventional modes of dress, the unprecedented phenomenon of "dropping out," especially among the children of the most successful classes, all have added their freight of disquiet and disconcert to the mood of our times.

When I call these causes of our present mood "topical," I do not imply that they are mere surface phenomena. Some of these manifestations may be no more than those curious societal epidemics that have often raged and then burned themselves out; others seem to have deeper roots and to signify changes of longer duration. By topicality I refer, rather, to the fact that these events have directly entered our daily lives, whether through newspaper headlines or by personal experience. They are events that have become part of our day-to-day existences, the conversational fare of a million breakfast tables, instilling in us a feeling of dismay, often bordering on despair.

I do not think, however, that we can account for our present mood solely in terms of these topical blows. Hence I call to our attention a second source of our present mood. This is a series of *attitudinal* changes that underlie and reinforce the topical events—changes that have not presented themselves as immediate existential concerns but have made themselves felt nonetheless as part of our inarticulated consciousness.

Somewhat arbitrarily, I select two of these attitudinal changes as being of central importance. The first is a loss of assurance with respect to the course of social events. The present generation of adults passed its formative years in a climate of extraordinary self-confidence regarding the direction of social change. For the oldest among us, this security was founded on the lingering belief in "progress" inherited from the late Victorian era—a belief suffused for some with expectations of religious or moral perfectibility, for others with more cautious but no less sustaining beliefs in the solid prospects for bourgeois society.

For the middle-aged, educated, as I was, in the 1930s, this Victorian heritage was already regarded as a period piece, battered first by World War I, then dealt its death blow by the Great Depression. But its comforting assurance had been replaced by an equally fortifying belief. This was the view that history, working like a vast organic machine, would produce a good socialist society out of a bad capitalist one. And for the younger adults, who formed their ideas in the 1940s and 1950s when this Marxian vista was itself regarded as an antique, reassurance was still provided by a pragmatic, managerial approach to social change. This was a time when one spoke of social problems as so many exercises in applied rationality: when economists seriously discussed the "fine tuning" of the economy; when the repair of the misery of a billion human beings was expected to be attained in a Decade of Development with the aid of a few billion dollars of foreign assistance, some technical advice, and a corps of youthful volunteers; when "growth" seemed to offer a setting in which many formerly recalcitrant problems were expected to lose their capacity for social mischief.

Today that sense of assurance and control has vanished, or is vanishing rapidly. We have become aware that rationality has its limits with regard to the engineering of social change, and that these limits are much narrower than we had thought; that many economic and social problems lie outside the scope of our accustomed instrumentalities of social change; that growth does not bring about certain desired ends or arrest certain undesired trends. One of these unmanageable events is the apparently unstoppable inflation that we witness in every industrialized capitalist nation. Another is the seemingly uncontrollable force of racial hatred, evident not only at home but in the relations of Hindus and Moslems, Jews and Arabs, Africans and Africans. Yet another is the stubborn resistance of world poverty to the ministrations of foreign aid, a phenomenon that we may perhaps understand better when we reflect on our inability to prevent the decline of some American cities into wastelands.

Hence, in place of the brave talk of the Kennedy generation of managerialists—not to mention the prophets of progress or of a benign dialectical logic of events—there is now a recrudescence of an intellectual conservatism that looks askance at the possibilities for large-scale social engineering, stressing the innumerable cases—for example, the institutionalization of poverty through the welfare system, or the exacerbation of racial friction through efforts to promote racial equality—in which the consequences of well-intentioned acts have only given rise to other, sometimes more formidable problems than those they had set out to cure.

Yet I do not believe that this second source of the erosion of confidence would by itself account for the pall that hangs over us were it not combined with another attitudinal change. This is our startled awareness that the quality of our surroundings, of "life," is deteriorating. Of all the changes in our background awareness, perhaps none is so important as this.

One aspect of this new awareness is a fear that we will be unable to sustain the trend of economic growth very much longer. The advent of an energy "crisis" alerts us to the prospect of a ceiling on industrial production, imposed by an inability to overcome the rapidly diminishing returns of a natural world that is being mined more voraciously each year. Such a prospect brings the troubling consideration of how we would manage the direction of events if economic growth—the central pillar of support for the sanguine views of Victorians, traditional Marxists, and managerialists alike—were forced to come to an early end.

But this prospect, though it may be the more immediate cause of our new-found concern with growth, is fundamentally less troubling than another recently recognized state of affairs. This is the stunning discovery that economic growth carries previously unsuspected side effects whose cumulative impact may be more deleterious than the undoubted benefits that growth also brings. In the last few years we have become apprised of these side effects in a visible decline in the quality of the air and water, in a series of man-made disasters of ecological imbalance, in a mounting general alarm as to the environmental collapse that unrestricted growth could inflict. Thus, even more disturbing than the possibility of a serious deteri-

19

oration in the quality of life if growth comes to an end is the awareness of a possibly disastrous decline in the material conditions of existence if growth does not come to an end.

Perhaps the combination of these topical and attitudinal elements is enough to account for the dark mood of our time. But I shall nevertheless advance a third reason, although I suspect it only flickers, so to speak, in our consciousness. It is a *civilizational* malaise that enters into our current frame of mind.

For some time, observers skeptical of the panacea of growth have wondered why their contemporaries, who were three or five or ten times richer than their grandparents, or great-grandparents, or Pilgrim forebears, did not seem to be three or five or ten times happier or more content or more richly developed as individual human beings. This skepticism, formerly the preserve of a few "philosophically minded" critics, has now begun, I believe, to enter the consciousness of large numbers of men and women.

The skepticism had a certain ring of hypocrisy so long as the great majority of men lived in a condition of low material attainment and static expectations. Only in the last century or so, as great masses of people have moved "up" the scale—each generation consuming food in quantity and quality superior to that of the classes above them in the preceding generation, each generation clothed in materials whose variety, color, fineness, and abundance surpassed the garb

20

of all but the very wealthiest figures of their youth, each generation able to enjoy a degree of mastery over death that would have appeared miraculous to its progenitors, each generation able to move about the surface of the earth or to command the powers of nature in ways that would have struck the previous generation with awe—only then could the warnings of the philosophers as to the ultimate inadequacy of material possessions be tested in reality and, after an initial period of euphoria, discovered to be true.

The civilizational malaise, in a word, reflects the inability of a civilization directed to material improvement—higher incomes, better diets, miracles of medicine, triumphs of applied physics and chemistry—to satisfy the human spirit. To say as much is not to denigrate its achievements, which have been colossal, but to bring to the forefront of our consciousness a fact that I think must be reckoned with in searching the mood of our times. It is that the values of an industrial civilization, which has for two centuries given us not only material advance but also a sense of *élan* and purpose, now seem to be losing their self-evident justification. As yet, the doubts and disillusions as to that civilization are only faint breezes that stir the leaves of the tree and will certainly not uproot a way of life anchored deeply in the earth of our beings. But the breezes blow and the stirrings they cause must be added to the sense of sometimes indefinable unease that is so much a part of our age.

It must be clear from these introductory remarks that I do not pose the question at the outset of this book—"Is there hope for man?"—as a mere rhetorical flourish, a straw figure to be dismantled as we proceed into more "serious" matters. The outlook for man, I believe, is painful, difficult, perhaps desperate, and the hope that can be held out for his future prospect seems to be very slim indeed. Thus, to anticipate the conclusions of our inquiry, the answer to whether we can conceive of the future other than as a continuation of the darkness, cruelty, and disorder of the past seems to me to be no; and to the question of whether worse impends, yes.

But all that remains yet to be demonstrated, or at least spelled out in some detail. And here we encounter a problem that must be faced before we plunge into the task of exposition. How are we to deal with the elements of wish and fear, prejudice and bias, charity and malice that come flooding into an inquiry such as ours, threatening to divert it, despite our best intentions, toward some outcome that we favor from the start?

The problem caused by the intrusion of subjective values into its inquiries has always troubled social science, which has struggled, without too much success, to attain the presumed "value-free" objectivity of the natural sciences. Alas, this ambition fails to take into account that the position of the social investigator differs sharply from that of the observer of the natural world. The latter may stake his reputation as he regards the stars through his telescope or the cells through his microscope, but he is not himself morally embedded in the field he scrutinizes. By contrast, the social investigator is inextricably bound up with the objects of his scrutiny, as a member of a group, a class, a society, a nation, bringing with him feelings of animus or defensiveness to the phenomena he observes. In a word, his position in society—not only his material position but his moral position—is implicated in and often jeopardized by the act of investigation, and it is not surprising, therefore, that we find behind the great bulk of social science arguments that serve to justify the existential position of the social scientist.

These difficulties must certainly affect an inquiry such as this one, not only on the part of myself, whose position, values, and interests shape and influence my perceptions, but equally on the part of the reader, who brings with him like considerations of social identification and similar vulnerabilities of moral posture.

To these difficulties I must add another, no less vexing. It concerns the "facts" toward which we must try to present an impartial and disinterested gaze. Unhappily, these facts are themselves a special problem for our inquiry. I shall try, of course, to base my argument on findings that will withstand the demolition of next year's research. But there is an aspect to the problem that goes beyond the obvious pitfalls in marshaling and weighing the evidence. It arises be-

23

cause much in our estimate of the human prospect must rest on generalizations for which there exist no objective data at all.

For the gravity of the human prospect does not hinge alone, or even principally, on an estimate of the dangers of the knowable external challenges of the future. To a far greater extent it is shaped by our appraisal of our capacity to meet those challenges. It is the flexibility of social classes, the resilience of socio-economic orders, the behavior of nation-states, and ultimately the "nature" of human beings that together form the basis for our expectations, optimistic or pessimistic, with regard to the human outlook. And for these critical elements in the human prospect there are very few empirical findings on which to rest our beliefs. We possess little or no "hard" information about the propensities of nation-states to peace and war, about the stubbornness or adaptability of social classes, or about the malleability of individual beings, except for those frail generalizations that we assemble from our real and vicarious life experience—itself biased, as we have said, by our situation within society and our private predilections. Thus, as regards the most important element of an effort to assess the prospect for man we have no guide but ourselves, and are thrown back, willy-nilly, to criteria that trouble us by virtue of their subjective foundation.

Here, as before, we encounter problems for which there is no solution other than the limited safeguards offered by self-scrutiny and a determined effort to subordinate our private interests to the superior claims of a "dispassionate analysis." I raise them, nonetheless, because I believe that not the least difficult part of an effort to discuss the human prospect is that of disengaging ourselves, either as partisans or as apologists, from the social situation in which we find ourselves, or from the social situation in which we could imagine ourselves in the future. Such considerations of self-interest may, and perhaps should, powerfully influence the point of view we take in advocating or opposing certain kinds of social change, but they can only play a distorting role when we try to stand aside from our private fates and reflect on the probable course of, and causes for, events, whether they are favorable for ourselves or not.

Talleyrand once remarked that only those who had lived in the *ancien régime* could know what "*les douceurs de la vie*" could be. He was referring to the *douceurs* of a court in which elegance and extravagance knew no bounds, and in which the wealthy and highly placed could indulge their whims and caprices with an abandon that we can only look back upon with the mixed feelings with which we regard the indulgence of all infantile desires.

In our period of history, however, it may well be that the threatened *douceurs* are those of an intellectual milieu in which the most extravagant and heretical thoughts can be uttered, if not in perfect safety (what society does not take *some* safeguards against its own destruction?), at least to a degree that has few parallels in history. Now let us suppose that the exigencies of the future, as we shall trace them out, point to the conclusion that only an authoritarian, or possibly only a revolutionary, regime will be capable of mounting the immense task of social reorganization needed to escape catastrophe. Might it not then be argued that the quasi-military devotion and sacrifice of such a task would be vitiated if the masses were exposed to the disagreements and diversions of intellectuals who strayed from, or opposed, the official line? Indeed, might not the people of such a threatened society look upon the "self-indulgence" of unfettered intellectual expression with much the same mixed feelings that we hold with respect to the ways of a vanished aristocracy—a way of life no doubt agreeable to the few who benefited from it, but of no concern, or even of actual disservice, to the vast majority?

I raise this issue not to debate its merits but to bring home as sharply as I can the kinds of defenses, arguments, and rationalizations to which our analysis will lead on more than one occasion. For were the necessary sacrifice not freedom of expression but freedom of acquisition, I imagine that a quite different set of emotions and individuals would be outraged.

Let me therefore forewarn the reader that he must be prepared to face problems in which values and beliefs precious to him may be assaulted by overriding

26

claims of human survival, and that he must therefore be prepared seriously to consider painful conclusions if he is not simply to substitute preference for analysis. Perhaps I should add that many conclusions in this book have caused great pain to myself, a fact which in no way vouches for their cogency but does at least argue that the human prospect, as I have come to see it, is not one that accords with my own preferences and interests, as best I know them.

TWO

The External Challenges

I HAVE SPOKEN so far of the "mood of our times" and of the personal considerations that make an appraisal of the human prospect so uncommonly difficult. But I have not yet set forth, except in the most general way, the nature of the challenges that we perceive in the world about us. As I have already indicated, the elements of danger in the human prospect are by no means all located in "external" threats, but in our "internal" capacity for response to those threats. Yet certainly the roots of our current anxiety spring in the first instance from dangers that we discern in the world around us, and it is therefore to these that our attention must first be addressed.

If we were asked to identify the principal "external" causes for the mood that assails us, I think that three aspects of the current human predicament would be unanimously selected. The first is a problem so well known that it has almost lost its power to shock, perhaps because attention has been focused largely on its humanitarian rather than its political implications. I refer to the demographic outlook for the next two to three generations.

31

An Inquiry into the Human Prospect

World population is today roughly 3.6 billion. About 1.1 billion live in areas where demographic growth rates are now tapering off, so that, barring unanticipated reversals in the trends of fertility and mortality, we can expect these areas—mainly North America, Western and Eastern Europe, Japan, Oceania, and the Soviet Union—to attain stable populations within about two generations. These stable populations will be approximately 30 to 60 percent larger than they are now, and this increase in numbers will add its quota of difficulties to the environmental problems facing mankind. But this ecological aspect of the human prospect, which we will examine later in this chapter, must be disentangled from the immediate problem of population overload.

The latter problem concerns the ability of those areas of the globe where population stability is not now in sight to sustain their impending populations even at the barest levels of subsistence. The dangers involved vary in intensity from nation to nation: there are a few areas of the underdeveloped world that are still underpopulated in their human carrying capacity. But in general the demographic situation of virtually all of Southeast Asia, large portions of Latin America, and parts of Africa portends a grim Malthusian outcome. Southeast Asia, for example, is growing at a rate that will double its numbers in less than 30 years; the African continent as a whole every 27 years; Latin America every 24 years. Thus, whereas we can expect

32

that the industrialized areas of the world will have to support roughly 1.4 to 1.7 billion people a century hence, the underdeveloped world, which today totals around 2.5 billion, will have to support something like 40 billion by that date if it continues to double its numbers approximately every quarter century.

Whether these horrific growth rates will in fact remain unchecked depends on two main variables. The first is the ability of the afflicted areas to introduce effective and stringent birth-control programs. Limited success in this regard has been enjoyed in a few places, mainly Taiwan and South Korea, although it should be noted that this "success" still leaves Korea and Taiwan among the fastest-growing populations in the world.[1] Almost no success has been attained in curbing growth rates in India or Egypt, despite official endorsement of population-control programs, and in those Latin American nations where growth rates are highest, population-control programs are not as yet even advocated. In fact, the only underdeveloped nation for which some cautious optimism may be voiced seems to be mainland China, where population-control programs, reportedly aimed at a zero growth rate by the year 2000, have been introduced with all the persuasive capability of a totalitarian educational and propaganda system.

Elsewhere in the underdeveloped world as a

1. See Kingsley Davis, "Population Policy: Will Current Programs Succeed?" *Science*, Nov. 10, 1967.

whole, population growth proceeds unhindered along its fatal course, with a virtual certainty of an 80 to 100 percent increase in numbers by the year 2000, and with projections thereafter that range between 6.5 billion and a grotesque 20 billion by the year 2050, depending mainly on estimates with regard to the rapidity of "spontaneous" or coerced changes in fertility.[2]

Still more alarming, even given the rise of governments of an efficiency and dedication comparable to that of China, a total curb on population growth appears to be impossible for the next century. This is because the fast-growing countries typically suffer from population age distributions in which almost half the population is below childbearing age. Therefore, even if drastic measures manage to limit families to a maximum of two children within a single generation, the steady advance of larger and larger numbers of individuals into their fertile years brings with it a vast potential increase in numbers. For example, if the underdeveloped countries were to achieve a zero population growth level of fertility by the year 2000, 50 years later they would nonetheless have increased in size two and a half times; if they succeed in achieving the target of "Western" fertility rates only by 2050, they will meanwhile have grown four and a half times in numbers.[3]

2. Tomas Frejka, "The Prospects for a Stationary World Population," *Scientific American*, March 1973.
3. *Ibid.*

For the next several generations therefore, even if effective population policies are introduced or a spontaneous decline in fertility due to urbanization takes effect, the main restraint on population growth in the underdeveloped areas is apt to be the Malthusian check of famine, disease, and the like. According to the 1967 report of the President's Science Advisory Panel on World Food Supply, malnutrition in the underdeveloped nations is already estimated to affect some 60 percent of their populations, with terrible costs in physical and mental retardation, while 20 percent suffer from undernourishment or actual slow starvation. All this contributes to preschool mortality rates three to forty times as high as those of the United States—a human tragedy of immense proportions, but also a demographic safety valve of great importance.

These Malthusian checks will exert even stronger braking effects as burgeoning populations in the poor nations press ever harder against food supplies that cannot keep abreast of incessant doublings. At the same time, the fact that their population "control" is likely to be achieved in the next generations mainly by premature deaths rather than by the massive adoption of contraception or a rapid spontaneous decline in fertility brings an added "danger" to the demographic outlook. This is the danger that the Malthusian check will be offset by a large increase in food production, which will enable additional hundreds of millions to reach childbearing age.

Here the situation hinges mainly on the prospects for the new "miracle" seeds, especially in rice and wheat, which have promised a doubling and tripling of yields. Fortunately or unfortunately, the future of the Green Revolution is still clouded in uncertainty. The new strains have not yet been adequately tested against susceptibility to disease, and there are suggestions from recent experience that they may be subject to blight. Perhaps more important in the long run is that all the new varieties of grains require heavy applications of water and of fertilizer. Water alone may be a serious constraint in many areas of the world; fertilizer is apt to prove a still more limiting one.

"Some perspective on this point is afforded," Paul Ehrlich writes, "by noting that, if India were to apply fertilizer as intensively as the Netherlands, Indian fertilizer needs alone would amount to nearly half the present world output."[4] Judging by the fact that of the 1.6 billion acres of currently cultivated land in the backward areas, less than 7 percent is now planted in the new seeds, a full "modernization" of agriculture would require enormous investments in fertilizer capacity. It is beyond dispute that these investments exceed by a vast margin the capabilities of the underdeveloped nations themselves, and it is possible that they exceed as well those of the devel-

4. Paul and Anne Ehrlich, *Population, Resources, Environment* (W. H. Freeman, 1972), p. 119.

oped world. More sobering yet, the introduction of fertilizers on such a scale may surpass the ecological tolerance of the soil to chemical additives.[5]

The race between food and mouths is perhaps the most dramatic and most highly publicized aspect of the population problem, but it is not necessarily the most immediately threatening. For the torrent of human growth imposes intolerable social strains on the economically backward regions, as well as hideous costs on their individual citizens. Among these social strains the most frightening is that of urban disorganization. Rapidly increasing populations in the rural areas of technologically static societies create unemployable surpluses of manpower that stream into the cities in search of work. In the underdeveloped world generally, cities are therefore growing at rates that cause them to double in ten years—in some cases in as little as six years. In many such cities unemployment has already reached levels of 25 percent, and it will inevitably rise as the city populace swells. The cesspool of Calcutta thus becomes more and more the image of urban degradation toward which the dynamics of population growth are pushing the poorest lands.

Only two outcomes are imaginable in this tragedy-laden historic drama. One is the descent of large portions of the underdeveloped world into a condition of

5. Barry Commoner, *The Closing Circle* (Knopf, 1971), pp. 84–93, *passim*.

steadily worsening social disorder, marked by shorter life expectancies, further stunting of physical and mental capabilities, political apathy intermingled with riots and pillaging when crops fail. Such societies would probably be ruled by dictatorial governments serving the interests of a small economic and military upper class and presiding over the rotting countryside with mixed resignation, indifference, and despair. This condition could continue for a considerable period, effectively removing these areas from the concern of the rest of the world and consigning the billions of their inhabitants to a human state comparable to that which we now glimpse in the worst regions of India or Pakistan.

But there is an alternative—and in the long run more probable—course of action that may avoid this dreadful "solution" to the overpopulation problem: the rise of governments capable of halting the descent into hell. It is certainly possible for a government with dedicated leadership, a well-organized and extensive party structure, and an absence of inhibitions with respect to the exercise of power to bring the population flood to a halt.

What is doubtful is that governments with such a degree of organization and penetration into the social structure will stop at birth control. A reorganization of agriculture, both technically and socially, the provision of employment by massive public works, and above all the resurrection of hope in a demoralized and apathetic people are logical next steps for any regime that is able to bring about social changes so fundamental as limitations in family size. The problem is, however, that these steps are likely to require a revolutionary government, not only because they will incur the opposition of those who benefit from the existing organization of society but also because only a revolutionary government is apt to have the determination to ram many needed changes, including birth control itself, down the throats of an uncomprehending and perhaps resistive peasantry.

Thus the eventual rise of "iron" governments, probably of a military-socialist cast, seems part of the prospect that must be faced when we seek to appraise the consequences of the population explosion in the underdeveloped world. Moreover, the emergence of such regimes carries implications of a far-reaching kind. Even the most corrupt governments of the underdeveloped world are aware of the ghastly resemblance of the world's present economic condition to an immense train, in which a few passengers, mainly in the advanced capitalist world, ride in first-class coaches, in conditions of comfort unimaginable to the enormously greater numbers crammed into the cattle cars that make up the bulk of the train's carriages.

To the governments of revolutionary regimes, however, the passengers in the first-class coaches not only ride at their ease but have decorated their compartments and enriched their lives by using the work and appropriating the resources of the masses who ride behind them. Such governments are not likely to view the vast difference between first class and cattle class with the forgiving eyes of their predecessors, and whereas their sense of historical injustice might be of little account in a world in which economic impotence also meant military impotence, it takes on entirely new dimensions in the coming decades for reasons connected with the changing technology of war. Thus a consideration of the population problem, as the first of the objective challenges of the human prospect, leads to an examination of the problem of war as the second of its imminent dangers.

What is new in the problem of war is, of course, the advent of nuclear weapons with their potential for "irreparable" damage, as contrasted with the much more restricted and more easily repaired damage of most conventional wars. As with the population problem, however, we are in danger of being rendered insensitive to the political ramifications of this element of danger in the human prospect by our tendency to picture it mainly in humanitarian terms.

The humanitarian aspect of nuclear war has focused our attention mainly on the stupendous killing power of the new weaponry. As Hans Bethe has described it:

Let us assume an H-bomb releasing 1,000 times as

40

much energy as the Hiroshima bomb. The radius of destruction by blast from a bomb increases as the cube root of the
increase in the bomb's power. At Hiroshima the radius of
severe destruction was one mile. So an H-bomb would
cause almost complete destruction of buildings up to a
radius of 10 miles. By the blast effect alone a single bomb
could obliterate almost all of Greater New York or Moscow
or London or any of the largest cities of the world. But this
is not all; we must consider the heat effects. About 30
percent of the casualties in Hiroshima were caused by flash
burns due to the intense burst of heat radiation from the
bomb. Fatal burns were frequent up to distances of 4,000 to
5,000 feet. The radius of heat radiation increases with power at a higher rate than that of blast, namely by the square
root of the power instead of the cube root. Thus the
H-bomb would widen the range of fatal heat by a factor of
30; it would burn people to death over a radius of up to 20
miles or more. It is too easy to put down or read numbers
without understanding them; one must visualize what it
would mean if, for instance, Chicago with all its suburbs
and most of their inhabitants were wiped out in a single
flash.[6]

Our horrified fascination with these and similar
statistics has led us to contemplate the consequences
of nuclear warfare in terms of the obliterative results
of using these weapons *en masse,* unleashing the
11,000 warheads now possessed by the United States
or the 1,200 or so warheads possessed by the Soviets.
Indeed, there are estimates of such an exchange, with

6. Hans A. Bethe, "The Hydrogen Bomb II," in *Scientific American Reader* (Simon & Schuster, 1953), pp. 194–95.

fatalities ranging from 50 to 135 million for the United States alone, depending on the defense "posture" of the various estimates.

It is understandable that we should be hypnotized by the vision of such ghastly possibilities. The risk, however, is that our concentration on this aspect of the consequences of nuclear warfare will lead us to overlook another result of the new technique of war. Essentially it resides in the fact that many small or relatively poor nations, even though they possess no fully developed industrial base or highly skilled labor force, can gain possession of nuclear weapons. As the example of China has shown, a nation with only a limited amount of industrial capacity can manufacture nuclear warheads by itself, although probably not missile delivery systems. The warheads can nonetheless be launched by bombers, smuggled into enemy harbors by ship, and so on. In addition, poor nations can obtain nuclear weapons as a by-product of the atomic power plants that many of them are now building or contemplating (or that will be built for them in the coming years by the developed countries).[7]

Thus there seems little doubt that some nuclear capability will be in the hands of the major underdeveloped nations, certainly within the next few decades and perhaps much sooner. The difficult question must then be faced as to how these nations might be tempted to use this weaponry. I will suggest that it

7. See Mason Willrich, "International Control of Civil Nuclear Power," *Bulletin of the Atomic Scientists*, May 1967.

may be used as an instrument of blackmail to force the developed world to undertake a massive transfer of wealth to the poverty-stricken world.

It may be, of course, that the governments of the underdeveloped world—and I would emphasize again the revolutionary cast of the governments that can be expected to arise in many places—will be able to arrange for the large-scale assistance they will need, and that they feel is owing to them, without recourse to these means. But given the reluctance to date of the developed world to offer more than token aid, and the likelihood that assistance on a scale large enough to raise the living standards of the six or eight billion of poverty-stricken inhabitants of the poor nations would necessitate an end to any advance, or even a decline, in the living standard of the well-to-do nations, the resort to ultimate tactics is surely not to be dismissed as a mere fantasy.

I do not raise the specter of international blackmail merely to indulge in the dubious sport of shocking the reader. It must be evident that competition for resources may also lead to aggression in the other, ''normal'' direction—that is, aggression by the rich nations against the poor. Yet two considerations give a new credibility to nuclear terrorism: *nuclear weaponry for the first time makes such action possible;* and *''wars of redistribution'' may be the only way by which the poor nations can hope to remedy their condition.*

For if current projections of population growth rates are even roughly accurate, and if the environmental limitations on the growth of output, to which we will turn in our next section, begin to exert their negative influences within the next two generations, massive human deterioration in the backward areas can be avoided only by a redistribution of the world's output and energies on a scale immensely larger than anything that has hitherto been seriously contemplated. Under the best of circumstances such a redistribution would be exceedingly difficult to achieve. Given the constraints on economic growth that will make their presence felt with increasing severity, such an unprecedented international transfer seems impossible to imagine except under some kind of threat. The possibility must then be faced that the underdeveloped nations which have "nothing" to lose will point their nuclear pistols at the heads of the passengers in the first-class coaches who have everything to lose.

Beyond the outlook for a dangerous rise in international tensions for the reasons we have discussed, this "scenario" cannot be further developed with any degree of confidence. Richard Falk has rather melodramatically extended the plot as a series of increasingly grim "decades": the 1970s characterized by a Politics of Despair; the 1980s by a Politics of Desperation; the 1990s by a Politics of Catastrophe; the Twenty-first century as an Era of Annihilation.[8]

I take this macabre prophecy as the worst, not the

8. Richard Falk, *This Endangered Planet* (Random House, 1971), pp. 420f.

most likely, possibility. Even if nuclear blackmail is used, it need not lead to global disaster unless it resulted in an unleashing of nuclear conflict among the great powers. It is more plausible that a terrorist attack—for example, the wiping out of a city in an advanced nation that had refused to pay a ransom of a large portion of its material output—would serve as a stimulus to bring a substantial reduction in nuclear armaments coupled with worldwide nuclear inspections, especially in the "dangerous" underdeveloped countries. Such a protective reaction would not reduce the chances for conventional limited wars—indeed, it might even increase them—but it would greatly reduce the risk of further nuclear threats of the kind we have described.

Unfortunately, even this happiest outcome to the immediate risks of nuclear catastrophe will not remove the influence of war as a fundamental molding element in the human prospect. As we have said, the danger of "limited" war remains, and the probability of such wars is very high. The frequency of "deadly quarrels" showed no signs of decline over the two centuries before 1940,[9] and experience in the past three decades is hardly encouraging: a casually assembled list includes civil conflicts in Greece, Korea, Nigeria, Pakistan, Indonesia, Sudan, and, on a smaller scale, Ireland; minor international sorties led by India,

9. L. F. Richardson, "The Statistics of Deadly Quarrels," in *The World of Mathematics* (Simon & Schuster, 1956), II, 1254.

Pakistan, England, France, Egypt, Israel, Portugal, China, and North Korea; major invasions conducted by the Soviet Union and the United States. Very probably wars on this scale, with this frequency of occurrence, will continue as long as nation-states continue to play their role as the main forms of mass social organization.

It is this last point that is of the essence. The continuing likelihood of war enters the human prospect not alone by virtue of the life-or-death risks it offers, but also as a principal reason for the continuation of nation-states as the dominant mode of social organization. The latter, in turn, gives unhappy assurance that nationalism, with all its potential for historic calamity, will be encouraged by the persisting realities of international existence—the omnipresent threat of war justifying the need for nation-states; the presence of nation-states in turn setting the stage for a continuance of the threat of war. From this vicious circle there is at present no escape, a fact that sets severe limits, as we shall see, on what one can expect by way of a fundamental response to many of the challenges ahead.

We shall return to the problem of the nation-state more than once in our subsequent chapters. But we cannot conclude this examination of the external dangers facing mankind without adding a third problem to those of population growth and war. This is the danger, to which we have already alluded, of en-croaching on the environment beyond its ability to support the demands made on it.

Here we come to a crucial stage of our inquiry. For unlike the threats posed by population growth or war, there is an ultimate certitude about the problem of environmental deterioration that places it in a different category from the dangers we have previously examined. Nuclear attacks may be indefinitely avoided; population growth may be stabilized; but ultimately there is an absolute limit to the ability of the earth to support or tolerate the process of industrial activity, and there is reason to believe that we are now moving toward that limit very rapidly.

When we examine the actual timetable of environmental disruption, however, we soon encounter a baffling set of considerations. Despite the certainty of our knowledge that a limit to growth impends, we have only a very imprecise capability of predicting the time span within which we will have to adjust to that impassable barrier. As we shall see, this makes it difficult to formulate appropriate policies, or to forecast the rate of social change that will be required to bring about the necessary environmental safeguards.

Take, as our initial problem, the availability of the resources necessary to sustain industrial output. In the developed world, industrial production has been growing at a rate of about 7 percent a year, thereby doubling every ten years. If we project this growth rate for another fifty years, it would follow that the demand for resources would have doubled five times, requiring a volume of resource extraction thirty-two times larger than today's; and if we look ahead over the ten doublings of a century, the amount of annual resource requirements would have increased by over a thousand times.

Do we have the resources to permit us to attain—or sustain—such gargantuan increases in output? Here the problem begins to reveal its complexity. A considerable proportion of the resources we extract today does not become industrial output but ends up as waste. To the extent that we can reduce waste, or use old outputs as new inputs—for example, recycling junked cars as new steel—we will be able to reduce the need for new resources, although by how much no one knows. Further, the problem is complicated because we are largely ignorant of the extent of most of the world's resources, petroleum being perhaps an exception. Indeed, not only is the world still largely "unexplored," so far as its potential mineral and other riches are concerned, but the very definition of a resource changes as our ability to extract minerals or other substances improves. For example, today we utilize enormous reservoirs of iron ore that were not even considered to be reserves when we were still mining the rich iron deposits of the Mesabi Range, now long exhausted. In point of fact, reserves of all known elements exist in "limitless" quantities as trace elements in granite or sea water, so that, given the appropriate technology and the availability of sufficient energy, no insurmountable barrier to growth need arise from resource exhaustion for millennia to come.

This conclusion depends, however, on several assumptions. It assumes that we will develop the necessary technology to refine granite or sea water before we run out of, say, "copper"—meaning copper in its present degree of availability.[10] More important yet, it assumes that the ecological side effects of extracting and processing the necessary vast quantities of rock or sea water would not be so deleterious as to rule out the new extraction technologies because of their environmental impact. Most important of all, as we shall see, the gigantic energy requirements for mining ordinary rocks or refining sea water bring us to the consideration of whether a continuously increasing application of energy is compatible with environmental safety.

To many of these questions no clear-cut answers exist. We do not know how rapidly new technologies of extraction or refining can be developed, or the degree to which anti-pollution technologies can suppress their ecological disturbance. Today, for example, the practical limit to open-pit mining, which appears to be the most economical way to extract

10. See T. S. Lovering, "Non-Fuel Mineral Resources in the Next Century," in *Global Ecology,* eds. John P. Holdren and Paul Ehrlich (Harcourt, Brace, Jovanovich, 1971); and Preston Cloud, "Mineral Resources in Fact and Fancy," in *Toward a Steady-State Economy,* ed. Herman Daly (W. H. Freeman, 1971).

49

common rock, is about 1,500 feet. It seems unlikely that this depth can be doubled, and it is a certainty that the rock extracted from such a vast pit will diminish exponentially unless ways can be found to dig pits with vertical walls.[11] In addition, as T. S. Lovering has written, "The enormous quantities of unusable waste produced for each ton of metal are more easily disposed of on a blueprint than in the field."[12]

But even if we make the heroic assumption that all these difficulties will be overcome, so that another century of uninterrupted industrial growth, with its thousandfold increase in required inputs, will face no constraints from resource shortages, there remains one barrier that confronts us with all the force of an ultimatum from nature. It is that all industrial production, including, of course, the extraction of resources, requires the use of energy, and that all energy, including that generated from natural processes such as wind power or solar radiation, is inextricably involved with the emission of heat.

The limit on industrial growth therefore depends in the end on the tolerance of the ecosphere for the absorption of heat. Here we must distinguish between the amount of heat that enters the atmosphere from the sun or from the earth, and the amount of heat we *add* to that natural and unalterable flow of energy by man-made heat-producing activities, such as industrial

11. Cloud, *op. cit.*, p. 61.
12. Lovering, *op. cit.*, p. 45.

combustion or nuclear power. Today the amount of heat added to the natural flow of solar and planetary heat is estimated at about 1/15,000 of the latter—an insignificant amount.[13] The emission of man-made heat is, however, growing exponentially, as both cause and consequence of industrial growth. This leads us to face the incompatibility of a fixed "receptacle," however large, and an exponentially growing body, however initially small. According to the calculations of Robert Ayres and Allen Kneese, of Resources for the Future, we therefore confront the following danger:

> Present emission of energy is about 1/15,000 of the absorbed solar flux. But if the present rate of growth continued for 250 years emissions would reach 100% of the absorbed solar flux. The resulting increase in the earth's temperature would be about 50° C.—a condition totally unsuitable for human habitation.[14]

Two hundred and fifty years seems to give us ample time to find "solutions" to this danger. But the seemingly extended timetable conceals the gravity of the problem. Let us suppose that the rate of increase in energy use is about 4 percent per annum, the world-wide average since World War II. At a 4 percent rate

13. W. R. Frisken, "Extended Industrial Revolution and Climate Change," E⊕S, American Geophysical Union, vol. 52 (July 1971), p. 505.

14. Robert U. Ayres and Allen V. Kneese, *Economic and Ecological Effects of a Stationary State*, Resources for the Future, Reprint No. 99, December 1972, p. 16. See also Frisken, *op. cit.*, and John P. Holdren, "Global Thermal Pollution," in *Global Ecology*.

of growth, energy use will double roughly every eighteen years. This would allow us to proceed along our present course for about 150 years before the atmosphere would begin to warm up appreciably—let us say by about three degrees. At this point, however, the enormous multiplicative effects of further exponential growth would suddenly descend upon us. For beyond that threshold, extinction beckons if exponential growth continues for only another generation or two. Growth would threfore have to come to an immediate halt. Indeed, once we approached the threshold of a "noticeable" change in climate, even the *maintenance* of a given industrial level of activity might pour dangerous amounts of man-made heat into the atmosphere, necessitating a deliberate cutting back in energy use.

In point of fact, serious climatic problems may be encountered well before that dangerous threshold. Noticeable perturbations are anticipated by climatologists when global man-made heat emissions reach only 1 percent of the solar flux, little more than a century from now.[15] This timetable assumes, however, that the rate of energy dissipation will not rise from its present rate of annual increase of 4 percent to, say, 5 percent or even higher. These estimates therefore make no allowance for *increases* in the rate of global heat dissipation if massive industrialization is under-

15. Frisken, *op. cit.*, p. 505.

taken in the underdeveloped regions. Per capita energy consumption in these areas is now only about one-tenth of that of the more advanced portions of the globe, although populations in the backward regions outnumber populations of the industrialized areas by two or three times. To raise per capita energy consumption in the poor regions of the world to Western levels would therefore require a twenty- to thirty-fold increase in energy use in these areas—a calculation that, however staggering, still fails to take into account the potential demands for energy from populations, within these areas, that will certainly double and possibly quadruple over the next hundred years.

It is important, in considering this last element of the human prospect, to avoid a prediction of imminent disaster. The timetable for global climatic disturbance is not only fairly distant, as we are accustomed to judge the time scale of events, but it can be pushed still farther into the future. Increases in the efficiency of power generation or utilization may considerably augment the amount of industrial production obtainable per unit of energy. New technologies, above all the use of solar energy, which adds nothing to the heat of the atmosphere since it utilizes energy that would in any case impinge on the earth, may greatly reduce the need to rely on man-made energy. From yet a different perspective, the technologies required to supplant the

53

present fossil fuels—safe and efficient fission reactors, economical solar or wind machines, large-scale geo-thermal plants—may not arrive "on time," thereby enforcing a slowdown in the rate of energy use and postponing the advent of an ecological Armageddon. More important, the vast energy sources required to "melt the rocks and mine the seas," notably fusion power, may also remain beyond our capability for a very long period, thereby curbing our fatal growth curve by depriving us of the needed resources. Finally, a wholesale shift away from material production to the production of "services" that demand far less energy would also greatly extend the period of safety—a possibility that we will look into in our next chapter.

Thus imminent disaster is not the problem here. It is the inescapable need to limit industrial growth that emerges as the central challenge. Indeed, the main lesson of the heat problem is simply to drive home with the greatest possible force the conclusion that such a limitation must sooner or later impose a strait-jacket on the never-ending growth of industrial production, even under the most optimistic or unrealistic assumptions with regard to resource availability or technology.[16]

The problem of global thermal pollution, for all its

16. I must add a footnote here, lest it be thought that the availability of safe solar energy obviates the problem of an energy constraint. Ayres and Kneese (page 51) point out that 250 years of growth, with its present associated emission of heat, would reach 100 percent of the total solar flux.

awesome finality, therefore stands as a warning rather than as an immediate challenge. Difficulties of a much more matter-of-fact kind—resource availability, energy shortages, the pollution resulting from noxious by-products of industrial production—are likely to exert their throttling effect long before a fatal, impassable barrier of irreversible climatic damage is reached. Every sign, however, points in the same direction: industrial growth must surely slacken and likely come to a halt, in all probability long before the climatic danger zone is reached.

Once again, however, we must stress an aspect of the environmental problem that is largely overlooked in the mounting literature on the ecological threat. Most of this literature focuses on the technical aspects of the problem, whose dimensions we have generally described. Of far greater importance for the human prospect are its socio-economic and political consequences. It is these aspects which will therefore mainly occupy us in the chapters to come.

There remains one concluding comment, before we proceed. At the outset I said that three elements of the current human predicament would be unanimously

---

It follows, therefore, that even the fantasy of a complete capture of all sunlight falling on the earth would yield no more energy than 250 years of growth of conventional (including nuclear) sources. Beyond that lies the exotic possibility of capturing additional solar energy in space and safely relaying it to earth by microwaves, or using microwaves to radiate man-made energy into space. The substantial application of such technologies seems far beyond any realistic capabilities of the next century or so.

55

selected if we were to seek the source of the pervasive unease of our contemporary mood. Now, without going beyond the specific dangers of population growth, war, and environmental deterioration, I must identify a fundamental element in the external situation—not so much a fourth independent threat as an unmentioned challenge that lies behind and within all of the particular dangers we have singled out for examination. This is the presence of science and technology as the driving forces of our age.

It is hardly necessary, I think, to spend much time defending the cogency of this unifying proposition. The population explosion that looms with such horrifying possibilities is directly traceable to the consequences of new techniques of science and technology in the area of medicine and public health: it is not a rise in fertility rates but a science-induced fall in death rates that has set off the unstable demographic situation that now threatens to overwhelm the underdeveloped areas. The responsibility of science and technology for nuclear armaments is self-evident, as is also their joint effect in bringing about both the rate of industrial expansion and the peculiarly dangerous nature of modern industrial processes. That science and technology may also be indispensable agents for the mitigation of these external dangers, through birth-control techniques, sophisticated means of arms detection or defense, or greatly improved methods of energy production and pollution suppression, does not vitiate the contention that these external dangers arise in the first instance because of the development of science and technology in that era we call "modern history."

The very possibility of using science and technology to mitigate our present problems indicates, however, that it is not the extraordinary development of these forces, as such, that underlies our predicament. It is, rather, their fusion in a civilization that has developed scientific technology in a lopsided manner, giving vent to its disequilibrating or perilous aspects without matching these ill effects with compensating "benign" technologies or adequate control mechanisms. In turn, this raises the question of whether scientific research and technological application follow their "own" courses of development, or whether these forces are imperfectly constrained and directed because of inadequacies of the economic and social milieu within which they have arisen.

That is a question for our next chapter. Here it is enough to claim that the external challenge of the human prospect, with its threats of runaway populations, obliterative war, and potential environmental collapse, can be seen as an extended and growing crisis induced by the advent of a command over natural processes and forces that far exceeds the reach of our present mechanisms of social control. It goes without saying that this unequal balance between power and control enters into, or provides the underlying basis for, that "civilizational malaise" of which I spoke earlier, and to which we will return.

At this point, however, we have still to push beyond the facts, as we can best identify and interpret them, to an analysis of their full impact on the human prospect. We have identified the external challenges; what remains to be examined is the response that can be mustered against these challenges—a response that now appears not alone in curbing or avoiding the specific threats we have mentioned but in coping with the dangerous tendencies of industrial civilization itself.

THREE

Socio-Economic Capabilities for Response

OUR LAST CHAPTER laid out for examination the external dangers of the human prospect. Yet that list of dangers still does not fully describe the challenge of the human prospect, nor wholly account for the somber state of mind with which we look to the future. For the dangers we have discussed do not descend, as it were, from the heavens, menacing humanity with the implacable fate that would be the consequence of the sudden arrival of a new Ice Age or the announcement of the impending extinction of the sun.

On the contrary, as we have repeatedly sought to emphasize, all the dangers we have examined—population growth, war, environmental damage, scientific technology—are *social* problems, originating in human behavior and capable of amelioration by the alteration of that behavior. Thus the full measure of the human prospect must go beyond an appraisal of the seriousness of these problems to an estimate of the likelihood of mounting a response adequate to them, and not least to some consideration of the price that may have to be paid to muster such a response.

The question is where to begin. Immediately two possibilities appear. The first is to discuss the question of adaptation and response in terms of our *individual* capabilities for change. This is an approach at once superficial and profound—superficial if it only leads us in the direction of moral exhortation or admonitions to change our behavior according to the dictates of reason; profound if it brings us to reflect on the ultimate capacities for individual change that may be rooted in what we call "human nature." The second possibility is to discuss the problem of response in terms of the flexibility of the social organizations that mobilize human effort and that powerfully influence human activity, in particular those massive social instruments for shaping behavior we call nation-states and economic systems.

I propose that we take the second avenue of analysis before the first, concerning ourselves in this chapter with generalizations and speculations about our collective capacity for response, and reserving to the next chapter various reflections on the problem of human nature.

This still leaves us with a choice of procedures. Shall we begin our consideration of the social capacity for action with an analysis of nation-states or with a discussion of socio-economic systems? For reasons that will become clearer as we go along, I shall again choose the latter, and, without further preamble, now broach the question of the adaptive properties of the two great socio-economic systems that influence human behavior in our time: capitalism and socialism.

Our choice of approach requires us to begin with the seemingly simple, but actually very difficult, task of making clear what we mean by "capitalism" and "socialism." If we begin with capitalism, I do not think there will be much disagreement as to the necessary elements that must go into our basic definition. Capitalism is an *economic* order marked by the private ownership of the means of production vested in a minority class called "capitalists," and by a market system that determines the incomes and distributes the outputs arising from its productive activity. It is a *social* order characterized by a "bourgeois" culture, among whose manifold aspects the drive for wealth is the most important.

As we shall see, this deceptively simple definition has unexpectedly complex analytical possibilities. But it also calls our attention to the necessity of conducting our inquiry at a suitable level of abstraction. It is the behavior of general socio-economic *systems* in which we are interested, not the behavior of particular examples of those systems. This is a consideration that has special relevance for the political animus that we carry with us in an investigation of this sort. It is a common tendency, for example, for radical analysts to assume that the word "capitalism" is synonymous with the words "United States." "The United States is a capitalist society, the purest capitalist society that ever existed,'' according to Paul Sweezy, the foremost American Marxian critic. Similarly, the French Marxist Roger Garaudy has agreed, ''The capitalist system in its most typical, richest, and most powerful expression, is that of the United States. . . .''[1]

Serious problems arise from the choice of the United States, not as the richest or most powerful, but as the *typical* capitalist nation. The first is the assumption that certain contemporary attributes of the United States (racism, militarism, imperialism, social neglect) are endemic to all capitalist nations—an assumption that opens the question of why so many of these features are not to be found in like degree in all capitalist nations (for instance, England or Sweden or the Netherlands), as well as why so many of them are also discoverable in non-capitalist nations such as the Soviet Union.

Second, the selection of the United States as the archetype of capitalism raises awkward issues with regard to socialism. For the logical question then is: If the United States is chosen to represent ''typical'' capitalism by virtue of its size, power, or global predominance, must we not designate the Soviet Union as the ''typical'' socialist nation for the same reasons?

1. Paul M. Sweezy, ''The American Ruling Class,'' in *The Present as History* (Monthly Review Press, 1953), p. 126; Roger Garaudy, *Marxism in the Twentieth Century* (Scribner, 1970), p. 13.

The radical critic recoils at this "logic," and explains the repugnant features of Soviet Russia as the unhappy legacy of its past, a tragic instance of the socialist ideal fatally compromised by the institutional and historical setting in which it was first achieved. But if we take this argument to be valid—and surely it has serious claim to consideration—are we not forced to extend the same apologia to the United States? That is, does not the United States then appear, not as a "pure" realization of capitalism, but as a deformed variant, the product of special influences of continental isolation, vast wealth, an eighteenth-century structure of government, and the terrible presence of its inheritance of slavery—the last certainly not a "capitalist" institution? Indeed, could we not argue that "pure" capitalism would be best exemplified by the economic, political, and social institutions of nations such as Denmark or Norway or New Zealand?

The point of this caution, which applies equally to the conservative who singles out the Soviet Union as the incarnation of socialism, is that we cannot analyze the adaptive properties of capitalism or socialism by confining our attention to the merits or shortcomings of any single example of either system. The range of social structures, traditions, institutions of government, and variations of economic forms is so great for both socio-economic orders that generalizations must be made at a very high level of abstraction—so high, in fact, that one may seriously question whether an analysis along these lines can shed much light on the adaptive capabilities of, say, "capitalist" Sweden or Japan versus "socialist" Hungary or East Germany.

Why, then, pursue at all the elusive question of the capabilities of these socio-economic orders? Two reasons seem cogent. First, the words "socialist" and "capitalist" continually recur in day-to-day (or in scholarly) discussions of the future, and therefore it seems worthwhile to examine the specificity that can be given to these terms, even if it turns out to be very small. Second, I believe a socio-economic analysis is warranted because, for all the variety in national forms, both systems must cope with common problems rooted in their economic and social underpinnings. That their responses may differ widely does not lessen the importance of singling out these common problems and examining the challenges they present to the family of related societies in which they appear.

Can we make a plausible prognosis with regard to capitalism as an "ideal type"?

Our first answer must be a disappointing one. On the basis of the bare specifications of capitalism two major historic projections for that system have been constructed, both of which have been demonstrated to be inadequate. The first of these projections lies along the lines of the Marxian "scenario" for capitalist development, a scenario foretelling its gradual polarization into two bitterly inimical camps, its growing inability to maintain a smoothly functioning economic process, and its eventual collapse through revolution. Central to that prophecy was the expectation that the dynamics of the system would create a working class "ever increasing in numbers," and disciplined by its economic hardships into an instrument of revolutionary historic change.

Some of that prediction, it should be noted, has been validated. The dynamics of capitalism did bring about a steady forced migration of farmers and self-employed small proprietors into the ranks of wage and salary workers, and the pronounced instability of the system did generate recurrent severe economic hardships. What seems to have forestalled the final vindication of the Marxian prognosis, however, was a series of developments that offset the revolutionary potentialities envisaged by its author. One such offsetting tendency was the steady augmentation of per capita output, which effectively undercut the development of proletarian feelings of exploitation. A related development was the rise of a "welfare" framework that also served to defuse the revolutionary animus of the lower classes. Last and perhaps most important was the gradual discovery—a discovery both in economic techniques and in social viewpoint—that government intervention could be used to prevent a recurrence of the near-catastrophic collapses suffered by the laissez-faire versions of capitalism characteristic of the late nineteenth and early twentieth centuries.

As we shall see, the Marxian conception of capitalism as a system inherently burdened with internal "contradictions" is far from being disproved by these events. But, meanwhile, what of the other major prognostication with regard to capitalism? Unlike the radical scenario, the second prognosis has had no single major expositor. It is to be found, rather, in the generally shared expectations of such writers as Alfred Marshall and John Maynard Keynes, or indeed the main body of non-radical twentieth-century economists.

Their prediction, like that of the Marxists, was also based on the presumed behavior of a private-property, market-directed, profit-seeking system, but not surprisingly it emphasized elements that were overlooked in the radical critique. The basic prognosis of the conservatives was that the capitalist system would display a steady tendency to economic growth, and that the socially harmful results of its operations —poverty, social neglect, even unemployment—could be effectively dealt with by government intervention within the institutional framework of private property and the market. As a result, the conservative view projected a trajectory for capitalism that promised the exact opposite of the Marxian: economic success coupled with a rising degree of social well-being.

Yet that prediction has also not fully materialized. As with the Marxian prophecy, certain of its elements were in fact attained, in particular an increase in per capita output and an expansion of social welfare policies. But the social harmony that was expected to result from these trends did not follow along. In the United States, for example, the economic transformation from the depressed conditions of the 1930s to those of the 1970s—a transformation that effectively doubled the real per capita income of the nation —failed to head off racial disturbances, an explosion of juvenile disorders among the affluent as well as among the poor, a widespread decay in city life, and a serious deterioration in national morale. And this disturbing experience has not been confined to the United States. Unprecedented economic growth in France and Germany and Japan has not prevented violent outbreaks of disaffection in those countries, especially among the young. Nor have Sweden and England and the Netherlands—all countries in which real living standards have vastly improved and in which special efforts have been made to reduce the economic and social distance between classes—been spared similar expressions of an underlying social discontent.

This failure of social harmony to accompany economic growth was as fundamentally disconfirming for the validity of the conservative prognosis as was the failure of a revolutionary temper to emerge for the radical prognosis. What explanation can we give? We can only hazard a few guesses. One is that poverty is a relative and not an absolute condition, so that despite growth, a feeling of disprivilege remains to breed its disruptive consequences.[2] Another is that each generation takes for granted the standard of living that it inherits, and feels no gratitude to the past.[3] Finally, the failure of the conservative prognosis may simply signal the possibility that whatever its economic strengths, the social ethos of capitalism is ultimately unsatisfying for the individual and unstable for the community. The stress on personal achievement, the relentless pressure for advancement, the acquisitive drive that is touted as the Good Life—all this may be, in the end, the critical weakness of capitalist society, although providing so much of the motor force of its economy.

The lesson of the past may then only confirm what both radicals and conservatives have often said but have not always really believed—that man does not live by bread alone. Affluence does not buy morale, a sense of community, even a quiescent conformity. Instead, it may only permit larger numbers of people to express their existential unhappiness because they are no longer crushed by the burdens of the economic struggle.

Does this confounding of two contrary prognoses leave us with anything on which to base a general estimate of capitalism as a system capable of meeting

2. See Richard Easterlin, "Does Money Buy Happiness?" *The Public Interest*, Winter 1973.
3. See Paolo Leon, *Structural Change and Growth in Capitalism* (Johns Hopkins Press, 1967), pp. 23f.

the problems of the future? We will be able to answer that question better after we have looked at the other side of the coin, and applied to socialism the same "ideal-typical" scrutiny that we have so far applied only to capitalism.

Here we must begin by recognizing a serious difficulty. In discussing capitalism as an ideal type, we had in mind a variety of "advanced" nation-states that, however different in many aspects, all shared a roughly similar social setting. Tacitly our analysis of capitalism referred to a group of nations characterized by a common "bourgeois" style of life and by highly developed industrial structures with their associated common aspects of mass production and high-level consumption.

When we turn to the consideration of socialism, no such unified image presents itself. We can easily describe socialism as an *economic system* by its replacement of private property and the market with some form of public ownership and planning. But socialism is much more difficult to specify as a social order than is capitalism. Indeed, we can identify at least two, and possibly three, social orders that rest on public property and planned economic activity.

One of these is typified by the industrial "socialism" of present-day Russia and much of Eastern Europe. Characteristic of this type of socialism are two salient features: an industrial apparatus closely resembling that of capitalism, both in structure and in outlook, and a highly centralized, bureaucratic, and repressive social and political "superstructure." A second "socialist" order is represented by the societies that have arisen in the underdeveloped world, or that are likely to emerge there in the future. Here political centralization and social repression exist, but not the framework of industrialism characteristic of the first type. This is the obvious consequence of present-day underdevelopment itself, but we must also consider the possibility that these nations will seek future development along lines that minimize such an industrial structure.

A third type of socialism presents far more difficulties for our kind of analysis than the other two, because it exists partly in historical fact, partly in imagination. This is a socialist order that seeks to combine a high degree of industrialism with a considerable amount of political freedom and decentralization of control. This form of socialism has been perhaps most closely approximated in the brief tragic career of "socialism with a human face" in Czechoslovakia and—to an extent difficult to determine—in contemporary Yugoslavia. More important, perhaps, is its existence in the minds of many socialist reformers as the kind of society toward which Western socialism may hope to move in the foreseeable future. It therefore exerts its influence as a historical force, even though its realization in fact is as yet very slight.

It will be necessary, therefore, to proceed with

great caution in attempting to describe the dynamics of the family of socialist societies. Nonetheless we can at least start with a striking fact. It is that the two main prognoses with respect to *industrialized* socialism have been proved as inadequate as did the corresponding prognoses with respect to industrial capitalism.

The first of these prognoses, frequently encountered only a generation ago, was that industrial socialism was "impossible," and that socialist economies would break down by virtue of their inherent irrationality. The resemblance of this prediction to that of the Marxian expectations with regard to the malfunction of capitalism is evident, and so is the failure of the prediction to come true. Despite the inability of industrial socialist economies to work with the smooth efficiency expected by their partisans—indeed, despite the frequent vindication of their critics' expectations of irrationality and malperformance—socialism did not break down. If economic discontent here and there reached threatening levels, the same can be said for the capitalist world in the 1930s. But in the one case as in the other, tendencies to growth overcame those of stagnation or crisis, so that by strictly economic criteria, industrial socialism proved as great a "success" as did capitalism.

But with the disappearance of the once confidently advanced prediction of a spontaneous collapse of socialist economies there also came a fading of a second prognosis, the counterpart to the sanguine outlook for capitalism. This was the belief that the replacement of private ownership by public ownership, and the displacement of the market by planning, would usher in an age of high social morale as well as high economic performance.

Again in striking parallel to the disappointments that have attended the growth of economic output under capitalism, the "successful" workings of socialist economic institutions have not brought the hoped-for results. On the contrary, if we are to judge by the relentless campaigns in the Soviet or East European press against absenteeism, carelessness, bureaucratic tyranny, or "un-socialist" attitudes, or by the actual revolts of workers in Poland and Hungary against their working conditions, or by the widespread evidence of a sense of intellectual oppression in many socialist nations, the social results of socialist economic growth have been very disappointing. If some of the more extreme forms of social disorder characteristic of the West, above all the anti-establishment mood and actions of youth, are much less to be observed, there seems good reason to credit this to the efficiency of the socialist police rather than to an absence of such tendencies on the part of the young. As evidence that these socialist nations have not generally attained their hoped-for level of communal spirit, there is the damning fact of the continuous efforts of their citizens at all levels of society to emigrate to capitalist nations, and the equally damning refusal of their authorities to permit the free entry of ideas.

These generalizations must, however, be more discriminatingly applied to "socialism" in general, with its range of types, than to the more unified cultures of bourgeois societies. In the underdeveloped nations, above all in China and Cuba, extraordinary efforts have been made to generate a high sense of morale, certainly with some success. We shall therefore look into the case of "under-developed" socialism more carefully in our next chapter. In Czechoslovakian or Yugoslavian socialism, the negative findings must also be tempered, although it is difficult to know by how much. But I think the evidence, even including these latter nations, is sufficient to enable us to assert that the economic success of industrial socialism, in and of itself, has not brought a corresponding rise in general "happiness" or social contentment, much as with the mixed record of economic success and social disappointment of capitalism.

I do not make this assertion to claim that industrial socialism has therefore failed: on the contrary, I imagine that in the minds of the majority of its citizens it has "succeeded," to much the same degree as capitalism. Rather, I call attention to the situation within the industrial socialist world to stress the surprising similarity of outcomes between two otherwise widely differing systems. Each has been marked with serious operational difficulties; each has overcome these difficulties with economic growth. Each has succeeded in raising its level of material consumption; each has been unable to produce a climate of social satisfaction.

75

This leads to the suggestion that common elements of great importance affect the adaptability of both systems to the challenges of the human prospect.

In the light of our analysis in the preceding chapter, it will not come as a surprise if I identify these common elements as the forces and structures of scientific technology on which both systems depend for their momentum. This suggestion would least seem to need supporting argument in explaining the ability of both systems to achieve economic growth, despite the malfunctions of the market in one case and of planning machinery in the other. All the processes of industrial production that are the material end products of scientific technology have one characteristic of overwhelming effect—their capability of enormously magnifying human productivity by endowing men with literally superhuman abilities to control the physical and chemical attributes of nature. Once an industrial system has been established—a historic process that has been as painful for capitalism as for socialism—it truly resembles a gigantic machine that asserts its productive powers despite the sabotage of businessmen or bureaucrats.

It is perhaps less self-evident that the common disappointments of capitalism and socialism with regard to the achievement of "happiness" can also be traced to the presence of scientific technology and the industrial civiliation that is built upon it. I have already pointed out the peculiar ills that may have their roots in the capitalist ethos, and it is also clear that many of the socialist dissatisfactions arise from the repressive political and social institutions to which we have called attention. Nevertheless, if we look more deeply I think we can find a substratum of common problems that spring from the industrial civilization of both systems.

For industrial civilization achieves its economic success by imposing common values on both its capitalist and socialist variants. There is the value of the self-evident importance of efficiency, with its tendency to subordinate the optimum human scale of things to the optimum technical scale. There is the value of the need to "tame" the environment, with its consequence of an unthinking pillage of nature. There is the value of the priority of production itself, visible in the care both systems lavish on technical virtuosity and the indifference with which both look upon the aesthetic aspects of life. All these values manifest themselves throughout bourgeois and "socialist" styles of life, both lived by the clock, organized by the factory or office, obsessed with material achievements, attuned to highly quantitative modes of thought—in a word, by styles of life that, in contrast with non-industrial civilizations, seem dazzlingly rich in every dimension except that of the cultivation of the human person. The malaise that I believe flickers within our consciousness thus seems to afflict industrial socialist as well as capitalist societies, because it is a malady ultimately rooted in the "imperatives" of a common mode of production.

I am aware, of course, that it is questionable to

77

assert that technology has "imperatives," for technology is no more than a tool in the hands of man. If the industrial apparatus has imposed its dehumanizing influence on capitalist and socialist industrial societies alike, there remains the possibility that in another milieu that apparatus could be turned to human account. It may be that extensive decentralization, workers' control, and an atmosphere of political and social freedom could better reconcile the industrial system with individual contentment.

I will not hide my doubts, however, that these reforms can wholly undo the de-humanizing requirements of an industrial system. Modes of production establish constraints with which humanity must come to terms, and the constraints of the industrial mode are peculiarly demanding. The rhythms of industrial production are not those of nature, nor are its necessary uniformities easily adapted to the varieties of human nature. While surely capable of being used for more humane purposes than we have seen hitherto, while no doubt capable of greater flexibility and much greater individual control, industrial production nonetheless confronts men with machines that embody "imperatives" if they are to be used at all, and these imperatives lead easily to the organization of work, of life, even of thought, in ways that accommodate men to machines rather than the much more difficult alternative.

The suggestion that a common industrial organi-

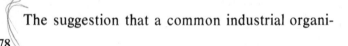

zation of life is responsible for certain parallels in the development of capitalism and industrial socialism can be no more than a speculation. More pressing are the immediate challenges that both great socio-economic orders will have to face.

We have already seen that the problem of population growth must be discussed in terms of the differential rates of growth of the developed and the underdeveloped lands. The question to be considered, then, is whether the dangerous consequences of the population problem in the underdeveloped world will, in the end, affect industrial socialist nations, such as the Soviet Union or East Germany, differently from capitalist nations, such as the United States or West Germany. These consequences, we will recall, resided in the encouragement given to the emergence of revolutionary regimes, and in the temptation—or necessity—for these regimes to use nuclear blackmail as a means of inducing the developed world to transfer its wealth on an unprecendented scale to the underdeveloped regions.

In this impending drama, it seems likely that the advanced socialist world will be the initial beneficiary of feelings of comradeship from the new revolutionary nations, and will probably be their immediate benefactor as well. Conversely, the rise of revolutionary governments presents the danger that capitalist nations will be tempted to use force to keep the spread of revolutionary socialism within bounds. The Indochina war, among whose motives the "containment" of communism was certainly a major element, is an all too clear example of precisely this form of counter-revolutionary activity. Thus, the population problem brings as an immediate consequence an aggravated risk of aggressive behavior on the part of the threatened capitalist world.

These reflections apply, however, mainly to the short run, when the setting of international existence will be much as we find it today. In the longer run the prospect alters considerably. To begin with, over a longer span we must resist the temptation to generalize from United States' belligerence in the past decade as firmly as we must resist similar generalizations based solely on the behavior of the Soviet Union. Looking over the record of capitalist nations during the past century, one does not discover a universal tendency toward military activity. The pacific attitude of the Scandinavian bloc, or of the smaller countries of Europe, the anti-military record of the United States until World War II (despite its punctuation by limited imperialist adventures), the recent disappearance of traditional warlike attitudes from the cockpit of capitalist conflict in Europe, make one cautious in declaring that capitalism is "inherently" a war-prone system. Moreover, in examining the motives that provoked the major capitalist wars during that century, one discovers, in addition to the specifically capitalist drives for economic expansion, powerful considerations of national prestige, strategic geographic advan-

80

tage, or simply ideological enmity—all motives that have driven nations long before the advent of capitalism as a system and that continue to manifest themselves visibly in the behavior of socialist nation-states.

More important yet, there is reason to believe that the pressures of the population explosion will come to bear increasingly on all nations alike, socialist as well as capitalist. The initial congruence of political interests between young revolutionary regimes and older industrial socialist ones must contend with a growing conflict over their economic aims. Given the closing vise of resource and energy supplies, and the gradually approaching barriers to growth imposed by the environment, it is clear that control over the planet's resources and claims on its output must become problems that will increasingly threaten the viability of all industrial systems. In the inescapable competition for dwindling resources and for the right to maintain, if not increase, the level of national output, I can see no reason why the imperatives of self-preservation should not operate as strongly among the socialist industrial nations as among capitalist ones. In both cases, wars of "preemptive seizure" would be a possible strategy. Barring such undertakings, I do not see why demands for a more equitable sharing of the world's output should not be as peremptorily directed by the poor countries against their rich socialist brothers as against their rich capitalist enemies.

The long-run problem then will be that of coping

with a "two-level" world. Whether or not that problem can be resolved without recourse to war, initiated by the poor countries or by the rich ones, cannot be foreseen. Much hinges on the degree of reason, compassion, or flexibility with which one endows the imaginary capitalist and socialist nations or ruling classes of the future, a matter in which our political presuppositions strongly affect our judgments.

This estimate need not be wholly subjective, however. For it becomes increasingly clear that the central issue of the future will lodge in the capability of dealing with the environmental limitations that emerge ever more insistently as the most intransigent of the problems of the future. Let us therefore ask what can be said as to the relative abilities of capitalist and socialist systems in coping with that challenge.

To start with the capitalist side, there is no doubt that the threatened depletion of resources, and the drastic ecological dangers that loom at a somewhat greater distance, directly threaten a main characteristic of capitalism—its strong tendency to expand output. This tendency serves three main functions for the system. It expresses the drives and social values of its dominant class. It provides the means by which a market-coordinated system can avoid the dangers of a "general glut." And, finally, it accommodates the striving of its constituents for larger rewards. Thus, expansion has always been considered as inseparable

82

from capitalism, whether as a necessary condition for its operation, as Marxian critics would claim, or as a justification for the institutions of private property and the market, as the conservative protagonists of capitalism have maintained. Conversely, a "stationary," non-expanding capitalism has always been considered either as a prelude to its collapse or as a betrayal of its historic purpose.

Is a stationary capitalism therefore unworkable? Is it a contradiction in terms? The answers are not open and shut, for they depend on various sociological assumptions from which, I need hardly add, our subjective evaluations cannot be wholly excluded. To begin with the first of the functions served by expansion, I do not think that one can make a dogmatic assertion that the social values and drives of its dominant class could not be accommodated within a largely static framework. Here we have the evidence of the extremely defensive economic posture characteristic of French or English capitalists just before and after World War II, respectively, and of the curiously bureaucratic complexion of Japanese capitalism, run by an extraordinarily "passive" and conformist managerial elite.

The expansive drive of capitalism springs, however, not only from the "animal spirits" of its dominant class but also from the restless self-aggrandizing pressures of its corporations. Here as well, however, a solution is imaginable. Much of the aggressive drive of firms arises from their continuous striving for a larger share of the market. A deceleration in growth, enforced by government decree, could include provisions for leaving market shares relatively undisturbed. Such a solution would be no more than a full-fledged transformation of "private" capitalism into planned "state" capitalism—a transformation already partially realized in Japanese capitalism.

It is perhaps less simple to construct a plausible stationary capitalism in the light of the second function served by expansion; namely, the avoidance of a severe economic crisis. As economists from Adam Smith and Marx through Keynes have pointed out, a "stationary" capitalism is subject to a falling rate of profit as the investment opportunities of the system are used up. Hence, in the absence of an expansionary frontier, the investment drive slows down and a deflationary spiral of incomes and employment begins.

Yet I do not think that one can maintain that a stationary capitalism is therefore "impossible." Expansion serves an indispensable purpose in maintaining a socially acceptable level of employment and demand in laissez-faire capitalism. It is by no means so certain that it is indispensable in a managed state capitalism. There seems no inherent reason why the deflationary tendencies of such a system could not be offset by a variety of measures. A high level of public demand could be provided by government investment in housing, education, and the like, by transfer pay-

84

ments within the nation, or by the distribution of "surplus" goods, if any existed, to the underdeveloped nations. All these measures are already in use in various parts of the capitalist world. Thus a stationary state would not seem to present insuperable problems for a managed capitalism, insofar as those problems concerned the maintenance of employment or aggregate purchasing power.

It may be argued that I have leaned over much too far in projecting such an optimistic prognosis for capitalist adaptation to a non-expansionary situation. I have done so deliberately, however, because there remains an aspect of the transition to a stationary system that strikes me as far more taxing with respect to capitalist powers of accommodation. This is the problem of finding a means of managing the social tensions in a capitalist system in which growth had ceased or was very greatly reduced.

Central to capitalism, as we have already noted, is a bourgeois ethos of economic advancement. Previously we have suggested that this ethos may be partly responsible for the failure of capitalist expansion to produce high social morale. But the pervasive values of competitive striving and expected personal advancement also present another problem—how to satisfy the demands of the lower and middle classes for higher living standards, while protecting the privileges of the upper groups. The solution has been to increase the output of the economy, thereby providing absolute

85

increases in income to all classes, while leaving the relative share of the upper groups relatively undisturbed.

The prospect of a stationary economy directly challenges this traditional solution. For under a stationary (or even a slow-growing) capitalism, continued efforts of the lower and middle classes to improve their positions can be met only by diminishing the absolute incomes of the upper echelons of society. A stationary capitalism is thus forced to confront the explosive issue of income distribution in a way that an expanding capitalism is spared.

In this connection we must bear in mind that we are not merely talking about the dismantling of a few vast fortunes or the curtailment of a handful of swollen incomes, although that might be difficult enough. What is at stake are the incomes of the upper middle classes, which include something like the upper fourth or fifth of the nation. This upper stratum is by no means composed of millionaires alone, but also includes teachers, shopkeepers, professional and technical workers: in the United States in the early 1970s a family entered the upper fifth with an income of about $15,000.

This stratum of society enjoys about 40 percent of the nation's total income. If the pressure from below were to eliminate its advantage over the "average" family, the upper stratum would have to yield a large fraction of its income, from perhaps a third at its lower levels to well over half at its upper levels. This gives one some appreciation of the magnitude of the political strain to which a massive pressure for income redistribution would give rise.

One saving possibility must, however, be considered in assessing this strain. It is possible that growth could be permitted to continue for an indefinite period, provided that it were confined to outputs that consumed few resources and generated little heat. An expansion in the services of government, in the administration of justice, in the provision of better health and education, arts and entertainment, would not only rescue the system from a fatal encounter with the environment but might produce enough "growth" to ease the income distribution problem.

If capitalism is to survive for a considerable period, this is the road along which it will assuredly have to travel. Perhaps in some cases it may successfully manage such a shift in the composition of its output. But we must not lose sight of the environment in which this shift must be made. A transition to a more equitable distribution of income within the capitalist nations will have to take place at a time when the larger struggle will focus on the distribution of resources among nations. If this struggle is gradually decided in favor of the underdeveloped world, whether out of humanitarian motives, the pressure of nuclear blackmail, or simply by the increased political cohesion and bargaining power of the poorer regions, the citizenries of the wealthy nations will find themselves in a long period of declining physical output per capita. This is apt to be the case, even without an international redistribution, if the many constraints of the environment exert their expected effects, beginning perhaps as soon as the coming decade.

Thus the difficulty of managing a socially acceptable distribution of income in the capitalist nations is that it will have to contend with the prospect of a decline in the per capita output of material goods. The problem is therefore not merely a question of calling a halt to the increasing production of cars, dishwashers, or homes while encouraging the output of doctor's services or the theater, but of distributing a shrinking production of cars, appliances, homes. The difficulties of a limited oil shortage have brought home to many Americans the hitherto unimaginable possibility that their way of life might not be indefinitely sustainable. If that shortage is extended over the next generation or two to many kinds of material outputs, a climate of extreme "goods hunger" seems likely to result. In such a climate, a large-scale reorganization of social shares would have to take place in the worst possible atmosphere, as each person sought to protect his place in a contracting economic world.

I am inclined to the belief, therefore, that the problem of income distribution would pose extreme difficulties for capitalism of a political as well as an economic kind. The struggle for relative position would not only pit one class against another, but also each against all, as lower and middle groups engaged in a free-for-all for higher incomes. This would bring enormous inflationary pressures of the kind that capitalism is already beginning to experience, and would require the imposition of much stronger control measures that any that capitalism has yet succeeded in introducing—indeed, than any that capitalist governments have yet imagined.

In bluntest terms, the question is whether the Hobbesian struggle that is likely to arise in such a strait-jacketed economic society would not impose intolerable strains on the representative democratic political apparatus that has been historically associated with capitalist societies.

It is of course, foolish to suggest that capitalism is the *sine qua non* of democracy, or to claim that democracy, with its commitment to political equality, does not conflict in many ways with the inequalities built into capitalism. Nonetheless, it is the plain historic fact that bourgeois societies have so far succeeded to a greater degree than any other social order in establishing parliamentary procedures, independent judiciaries, and constitutionally limited executives, all essential elements in a democratic political system. The question to be faced, then, is whether these political institutions can be expected to cope with the social and economic transformations whose extensive character we have indicated.

Here prediction along the lines of an "ideal type"

cannot bring us very far. It is possible that some capitalist nations, gifted with unusual political leadership and a responsive public, may make the necessary structural changes without surrendering their democratic achievements. At best, our inquiry establishes the approach of certain kinds of challenges, but cannot pretend to judge how individual nations may meet these challenges. For the majority of capitalist nations, however, I do not see how one can avoid the conclusion that the required transformation will be likely to exceed the capabilities of representative democracy. The disappointing failures of capitalist societies to create atmospheres of social harmony, even in expansive settings, does not bode well for their ability to foster far-reaching reorganizations of their economic structures and painful diminutions of privilege for their more prosperous citizens. The likelihood that there are obdurate limits to the reformist reach of democratic institutions within the class-bound body of capitalist society leads us to expect that the governments of these societies, faced with extreme internal strife or with potentially disastrous social polarization, would resort to authoritarian measures. To the extent that these measures would necessarily include the national management of corporations and the non-market determination of income levels, the direction of change might be described as a movement toward "socialism," although in a manner very different from that of the classic revolutionary scenario and with implications that will distress the partisans of socialism as a democratic form of government.

These reflections raise a question that may have been impatiently waiting in the reader's mind. After all, the ecological threat is still some distance in the future. Hence long-term speculations as to the feasibility of a stationary capitalism may seem hopelessly academic in the face of nearer-terms risks of war, or of the disruption of capitalism from other causes, such as its inability to generate a high enough social discipline and morale. That may indeed be the case. But if capitalism collapses, what next?

As we have already seen, the successor may well be a severe authoritarian regime that is not easy to analyze in terms of our socio-economic ideal types. But let us suppose that the collapse of capitalism would usher in socialism—that is, a society built on the public ownership of goods and the replacement of the market by widespread planning. What can we say about the capabilities of such a system before the demands of the environmental challenge?

Here the possibilities of applying a socio-economic analysis seem much simpler. It appears logical to conclude that socialism, with its direct commitment to a planned economy and with its freedom from the ideological blockages of private property, could manage the adaptation of an industrial society to a stationary equilibrium much more readily than capitalism.

I believe this is true in the short run. Over a longer period, however, grave problems would emerge. A socialist society would also have to achieve a politically acceptable distribution of its income among its people. The task of arriving at such as division of income would be much more difficult in a period of shrinking physical output than in an economy where all levels expected their real incomes to rise. Hence a democratically governed socialism would very likely face the same Hobbesian struggle for goods as a democratically governed capitalism; and whereas an authoritarian socialism could certainly enforce some kind of solution, it seems likely that this would entail a degree of coercion that would make "socialism" virtually indistinguishable from an authoritarian "capitalism."

The similarity of the problems of and responses to the stationary state for both socialism and capitalism brings us finally to confront a question that has persisted like a *basso ostinato* through these pages. This is the relation of the two systems to the industrial civilization that has again and again emerged as a root cause for the dangers of the human prospect and as the common basis for the economic successes (and perhaps the social failures) of capitalism and industrial socialism. Is it now possible to maintain, on the grounds of our socio-economic analysis, that socialism will have a significant advantage over capitalism in asserting the necessary controls over the runaway forces of science and technology?

Once more I believe we must differentiate between the short-run and long-run capacities for response. In the short run, as in the case of international tensions and in the initial stages of coping with the pressures of a stationary economy, I would think that industrial socialism would possess important advantages. The control over the direction of science, over its rate of incorporation in technology, and over the pace of industrial production as a whole should be much more easily achieved in a society that does not have to deal with the profit drive, than in one that does. To be sure, socialist systems have their own handicaps in the bureaucratic inertias of planning. But the absence of a necessity to heed the pull of commercial considerations should nonetheless confer an additional degree of social flexibility to the socialist control over the industrial process.

In the longer run, however, I believe that we find a convergence of problems, as we have so often before. For what portends, in that longer run, is a challenge of equal magnitude for industrial socialism as for capitalism—the challenge of drastically curtailing, perhaps even dismantling, the mode of production that has been the most cherished achievement of both systems. Moreover, that mode of production must be abandoned in a mere flash of time, as historic sequences are measured. Given the present pace of industrial growth—which will take prodigies of science to maintain in the face of dwindling resources—the edge of the heat emission danger zone may be reached in as little as three or four generations. Failing the achievement of the needed scientific break-throughs, we will be spared the heat barrier simply because we will be unable to produce the emergy or to process the resources to maintain our present growth rates.

Thus, *whether we are unable to sustain growth or unable to tolerate it*, there can be no doubt that a radically different future beckons. In either even-tuality it seems beyond dispute that the present orien-tation of society must change. In place of the long-established encouragement of industrial production must come its careful restriction and long-term dimi-nution within society. In place of prodigalities of consumption must come new frugal attitudes. In these and other ways, the "post-industrial" society of the future is apt to be as different from present-day indus-trial society as the latter was from its pre-industrial precursor.

Can we expect an industrial socialist society, be it characterized by authoritarian or by democratic gov-ernment, to weather such a transformation more easily than a capitalist society, "private" or state? I doubt it. Both socio-economic systems are committed to a civi-lization whose most striking aspect is its productive virtuosity. But my skepticism is based on more than the resistances and inertias of vested interests that we find throughout history when established modes of production become obsolete. It is also founded on a political consideration, namely, whether *any* society can bring about alterations of this magnitude through the conscious intervention of men, rather than by convulsive changes forced upon men. I cannot hope to substantiate this judgment until we have looked into the political and psychological dimensions of the human capacity for response. This is the aspect of the human prospect to which we must therefore now turn our attention.

FOUR

The Political Dimension and "Human Nature"

OUR LENGTHY ANALYSIS OF capitalism and Western socialism has led to one principal conclusion: the dangers of the human prospect seem likely to affect the two systems differently in the short run, but surprisingly alike over a longer time horizon. As we have seen, this conclusion rests on the central place which we have assigned to industrial technology, the source of social and economic pressures that impose common problems on both social orders, regardless of their different institutions and ideologies. Beyond that conclusion, however, our analysis becomes blurred. The logic of socio-economic analysis takes us a certain distance, and then leaves us with a sense of indeterminacy and incompletion.

The reason is clear enough. Our inquiry has been entirely conducted by tracing out the "logical dynamics" of a system of profit-seeking firms and individuals, or of efficiency-minded ministries of production. What we have omitted has been any consideration of a political dimension—that is, any systematic introduction of the problem of political power, either in terms of the "logical dynamics" of the behavior of nation-states or of those imperatives of behavior or capacities for response that involve the rather ill-defined areas of life we call "political."

The reasons for this omission, in turn, are easy to understand. We live in an age in which the very capacity for socio-economic analysis marks us off from the past. We read with amusement or shock the historical prognoses of the classical historians or political philosophers, into which socio-economic dynamics do not enter at all (for the very good reason that the relevant social systems had not yet evolved) and in which, instead, we find purely political predictions, usually of dynastic rise and fall, and so forth. But however more "scientific" our socio-economic method may seem by comparison, its omission of a political dimension is nonetheless crippling, even fatal, for a comprehension of the human prospect.

For the exercise of political power lies squarely in the center of the determination of that prospect. The resolution of the crises thrust upon us by the social and natural environment can only be found through political action. The dependence of the under-developed nations on strong governments has been sufficiently emphasized not to need repetition here. But the very same considerations apply to the nations of the developed world. Here too the most active use of political power will be inescapable, in part as a

100

necessary response to any threats directed at them by the underdeveloped world, in part as the only means to meet and control the challenges of a threatening environment. Certainly the expansive thrust of a market system can be contained and coordinated only by the direct assertion of a greatly expanded domestic national power, as we have indicated; and it is hardly necessary to rehearse the similar conclusions that we reach for industrial socialist nations. As David Calleo and Benjamin Rowland write: "The nation-state may all too seldom speak the voice of reason. But it remains the only serious alternative to chaos."[1]

It is one thing, however, to determine that a political dimension must be added to socio-economic analysis; it is another to provide that dimension. For what is there to be said about the exercise of national power that can compare with the "logical dynamics" of socio-economic reasoning? The classical historians unblushingly likened the course of national history to the life of man, writing of the youth, middle age, and dotage of nations, or took for granted the "human nature" that made the behavior of princely states as predictable as that of man. But we cannot accept the metaphorical comparisons or the psychological assumptions of these philosophers. What is then left to put in their place? What can be said predictively, or even analytically, about the use of political power?

1. *America and the World Political Economy* (Indiana University Press, 1973), p. 191.

At the outset we must recognize that there is an aspect of the political dimension that totally eludes our grasp; alas, a vitally important aspect. When we look to the political future to foresee the specific deployment of political power, we are in even greater ignorance than the classicists, who at least thought they knew how men behaved, schemed, and responded with respect to power. We know only that we cannot predict the idiosyncratic behavior of national leaders and therefore cannot foresee the national behavior that is still so much the lengthened shadow of individual leaders. We cannot even predict mass phenomena, such as the "flash points" at which political discontent turns into revolution, or the probabilities that any given regime will muster the support of the people. Thus, over large and critical areas of political behavior, both among and within nations, we are thrown back on our intuitions, hunches, or "wisdom," sometimes presciently, more often not.

But that is not quite an end to it. If the boldest and most far-reaching exercise of political power will be unavoidable over the future, this does more than introduce a random element about which nothing can be said. It also raises the question of whether this exercise of power will be successful, in the sense that it will be accepted by those over whom that power will have to be exercised. *One cannot have political power without political obedience; one cannot have strong government without a sense of national identification.*

How do we know that the use of power, which emerges as such a central necessity for the survival of mankind, will be in fact accepted? What can we say about those traits of political obedience and national identification that we suddenly discover to be the preconditions for the effective mobilization and use of power, whether for evil ends or for life-saving ones?

Here, fortunately, we are not quite in the dark. For the behavioral traits that "permit" the use of political power lie within our scrutiny, even to a certain extent within our predictive capabilities. Therein lies, therefore, the direction in which we must go if we are to introduce the missing political dimension into our inquiry.

Such an effort takes us in the direction of that shadowy concept we call "human nature," but along a very different route from that of the classical historians. We are interested in an examination of man that may throw light on certain attributes of his political behavior. Hence we must begin by focusing our attention on a central fact of human existence—the extended period of helplessness and development through which all human beings must pass and in which the elements of their adult personalities are first molded.[2]

The essential features of this crucial period are

2. For a similarly oriented study, see Harold D. Lasswell, "The Triple-Appeal Principle: A Contribution of Psychoanalysis to Political and Social Science," *American Journal of Sociology*, Jan. 1932.

familiar from the work of Freud and his successors, and can be rapidly summed up. As an infant, still unable to move, the human being experiences (as best we can imagine its scarcely formed consciousness) a sense of infantile omnipotence, in which it "believes" that the world is only an extension of itself, responding to its cries with food, warmth, tactile support, and so on. Moreover, if this "belief" were not in fact based on reality, the infant would perish. Later, as the infant begins to recognize the independent existence of an outer world, it gains the frightening awareness that far from being omnipotent, it is virtually powerless, literally dependent for life itself on the ministration of adults over whom it has no control whatsoever. Later still, as the child seeks to control and direct its physical and psychic energies, it learns to model its behavior on that of adults whose presence is still indispensable and whose wills are irresistible.

In this universal crucible of experience, as we well know, are forged those tendencies in the human personality that later reveal themselves in various sexual, intellectual, aesthetic, moral, and other attitudes. What interests us here, however, are those aspects of the conditioning process that find their vent in the traits of obedience and the capacity for identification—the necessary preconditions for the successful functioning of political institutions in mobilizing individuals for tasks of both peace and war.

The first of these "political" aspects of "human

nature"—the trait of obedience—is surely simple enough to locate in the first few years of experience. What is perhaps less obvious is its expression in adult behavior. The phenomenon to which I wish to call attention is the normal willing acquiescence of men in the exercise of political authority itself. The nature of the "legitimacy" of this authority has been, of course, the object of an extensive discussion, emphasizing such purposes as the preservation of property, the conduct of war, the establishment of law, or, in our own case, the safeguarding of a society threatened by the environment. I have no intention of entering further into this area of "functional" political analysis. Rather, I wish to stress an aspect of political authority that may be obscured by an exclusive concentration on its objective purposes. This latent function is to provide a sense of psychological security by re-creating the accustomed relationships of sub- and superordination to which our long period of helpless dependency has accustomed us.

Certainly we find evidence of this in the ascription of majesty to kings and queens, who are obvious substitutes for our parents, or in the childlike attitudes of mingled resentment and admiration with which the lower orders of society characteristically regard the higher orders, or in the "cult of personality" to which the peoples of the world show such willingness to succumb. Anyone who has seen the wild excitement of a crowd caught up in the adulation of a political leader cannot fail to recognize the rekindling of child-hood feelings of awe and obedience in the behavior of these cheering adults.

I am aware, of course, that I tread here on danger-ous ground. The experience of childhood is also the source of those drives for self-assertion that contend with obedience, both during and after childhood. Further, it is apparent that the conditioning experience imparts only a very general "tendency" toward obedi-ence—one that finds manifold expressions in adult political behavior, as the most cursory examination of political life reveals in, say, England and Italy.

Nor does a stress on the biopsychological under-pinnings of political submissiveness deny the impor-tance of other elements which are inextricable from the acquiescence in power. One of these is the presence of force, overtly or covertly employed by the ruling elements to establish and maintain their authori-ty. Another is the differential social conditioning to which different classes in society are exposed. Still another may be the unequal distribution of personality characteristics that lead to power and submission. At still a different level are the hierarchical orderings we observe in many other species.

Nevertheless, a ready admission as to these, or still other, more "positive" reasons for the acceptance of political authority does not explain the phenomenon to which my speculations are addressed. This is the perplexing readiness, even eagerness, with which authority is accepted by the vast majority. An acquiescence, in, or search for, a hierarchical ordering includes not only the lower and middle reaches but also the upper levels of society, who regularly look for "leadership" to someone still higher in the world. Indeed, it finds striking expression in the habit of rulers, including the most dictatorial and absolute, to declare their own "submission" to a will higher than their own, whether it be that of God, of "the people," of some sacred text or doctrine, or of voices audible to themselves alone.

This line of thought has several consequences for the political dimension of the human prospect. To begin with, it offers a substantive basis for our view that the problem of political power exists, not as a mere epiphenomenon of socio-economic relationships, but as a "reality" in its own right whose roots and characteristics can be, at least to some extent, analyzed and applied to the general prognosis for mankind.

In turn this argument has special relevance for several matters we have encountered. One of these is the political outlook for revolutionary socialism, among whose aims is a desire to destratify society to an unprecedented degree. As the example of China illustrates, there is no reason to doubt that impressive changes can be achieved in lessening the social or economic gradations among classes or individuals. But it is useful to consider that the Chinese effort to minimize social and economic hierarchies has taken place within a political framework whose over-all hierarchical structure is as pronounced as that of any society in history. The virtual deification of Mao has made China very nearly a personal theocracy, and its striking egalitarian achievements must therefore be viewed in the context of a political order that satisfies the hunger for authority by concentrating it on one remarkable order-bestowing figure. If our speculations are justified, it would follow that revolutionary regimes will be able to perpetuate extreme egalitarian structures only through a succession of leaders endowed with tremendous authority, or else must move in the direction of reestablishing the legitimacy of relations of authority that are now regarded as violations of the revolutionary spirit.

Further, our analysis affords some understanding of the difficulties of democratic governments in managing social tensions. As the histories of the United States, or Switzerland, or modern Scandinavia all illustrate, democracies can provide stable and strong government that assuredly offers some satisfaction for the "political hunger" of mankind. Yet, even in these cases, strong leaders provide a sense of psychological well-being that weak ones do not, so that in moments of crisis and strain demands arise for the exercise of strong-arm rule. As the histories of ancient and modern democracies illustrate, the pressure of political movement in times of war, civil commotion, or general anxiety pushes *in the direction of authority,* not away from it. These tendencies may be short-lived, or may give rise to totalitarian governments that in time collapse, but I do not think that one can deny that these pressures are a persistent fact of political life. One reason for them may indeed lie in the belief— itself perhaps a consequence of the phenomenon of conditioned obedience—that centralized authority will cope with crisis and unrest more "successfully" than less authoritarian structures. But another reason, I venture to suggest, lies in the capacity of powerful "parental" figures, successful or not, to re-create the emotional and psychological custody of one's early years.

I am acutely conscious that this general line of arguments smacks of the worst kind of reactionary ideology: one of the most familiar excuses for dictatorship is that the masses are "children" and must be treated as such. Nonetheless it would be foolish, as well as hypocritical, not to admit that tendencies toward authoritarian rule seem to be a chronic feature of political life: how many egalitarian revolutions have not ended in the creation of a political establishment every bit as authoritarian as that which they originally displaced? It behooves us therefore to understand this "logic" of political behavior as well as possible, particularly in view of the extraordinary difficulties with which democratic governments will be faced in the coming decades and generations.

Finally, and with great reluctance, I must advance one last implication of my argument. It is customary to recognize, but to deplore, the authoritarian tendencies within civil society, especially on the part of those who, like myself, are the beneficiaries of the freedoms of minimally authority-ridden rule. Yet, candor compels me to suggest that the passage through the gantlet ahead may be possible only under governments capable of rallying obedience far more effectively than would be possible in a democratic setting. If the issue for mankind is survival, such governments may be unavoidable, even necessary. What our speculative analysis provides is not an apologia for these governments, but a basis for understanding the critical support that they may be able to provide for a people who will need, over and above a solution of their difficulties, a mitigation of their existential anxieties.

Let me now advance a second suggestion with regard to the psychological underpinnings of political life. As we have already said, this element concerns the capacity for identification—and in particular *national* identification—which is, like the adult sublimation of childhood obedience, an indispensable precondition for the exercise of political action.

This second political element in "human nature" also finds its origins in the universal conditioning period when the very young child draws its strength and security from those familial figures with whom it min-

110

gles its own identity. From this identificatory capacity of the child there flowers, in adult life, an extraordinary array of behavior traits, ranging from the merging of one's self with one's possessions to the capacity for love and sympathy and fellow-feeling. Indeed, the generalized capability of identification is the soil in which are rooted all possibilities of morality.

But we are interested here in the specifically "political" behavior traits that can be traced to this elemental human attribute, and now we find a striking fact. Although the capacity to empathize widens and becomes ever more disciminatingly applied as the child grows older, within every culture of which I have knowledge there seems to be a limit beyond which this general identificatory impulse is blocked. This limit divides those within a society from those beyond it, and demarcates the members of a group among whom a shared concern exists, even though the members may be unknown to one another, from those for whom no such concern is felt.

Once again, it seems possible to trace this otherwise inexplicable fact to the persistence of early childhood attitudes. The child divides the world into two—one comprised of its original family and its subsequent extension of that family; the other of non-familial beings who may exist as human objects but not as human beings with whom an identificatory bond is possible. These same attitudes persist in the political phenomenon of "peoplehood," a phenomenon we find in every culture, ancient and modern. For reasons that we do not fully understand but must accept as a patent fact, nation-states—often with the most hetero-geneous populations—can serve as psychologically valid surrogates for the family and therefore as the beneficiaries of a powerful uniting bond that enables national authorities to concert the actions of diverse individuals. Equally important, nations (or other groups such as tribes or clans) also evidence the limita-tions to the bond of identification, and look upon mem-bers of other states or groups with the same unseeing eye that the child fastens on someone who is merely an object and not a person.

The implications of these remarks for the problem of political prognosis seem clear enough. The feeling of national identity adds another independent under-pinning to the suggestion that the nation-state must be considered as the embodiment of purely political, as well as socio-economic, behavioral forces. Once again this suggestion bears with special relevance on the prospects for revolutionary socialism. For all their socio-economic doctrinal orientation, revolutionary movements most effectively attain their capacity to unite and motivate people when they are welded to the unifying political capabilities of the state. This welding helps us understand the tendency of revolutionary movements, such as the Cuban or Chinese, to infuse their socio-economic teachings with patriotic flavor, together with authoritarian elements of catechism and unimpeachable moral prerogatives. Much of the success of such revolutionary efforts therefore depends on appeals to "primitive" elements—a comment in no way intended to downgrade the actual improvements that these revolutions may bring but to help us understand the nature of the motives on which they are forced to rely.

On a larger scale, the power of the political fantasy in drawing boundaries between those who matter and those who do not carries its disquieting freight for the human prospect in general. For this manifestation of the political element in "human nature" makes it utopian to hope that we will face the global challenges of the future as an international brotherhood of men. If it were possible to imagine the future in terms of the expectations of the 1950s—a "manageable" world in which expert administration would gradually replace the clumsy ignorance of the past—one could hope that the demarcative power of national identification would gradually recede before a kind of international fraternity of administrators and technicians.

The mounting tensions and eventual major transformations that await industrial societies greatly weaken that fond hope. Given the magnitude of the changes that we have sketched out and the competitive struggle for existence that portends, it is unlikely in the extreme that mankind will enjoy a setting in which the identificatory potential within "human nature" can be extended to embrace men and women of other "peoples," or that considerations of a pan-numanistic kind will displace the narrowly familistic basis on which identification is today founded.

For all these forebodings, it is important to recognize that nationalism, despite its potentially vicious application, is not solely a destructive force, and that political identification, with all its problems, is by no means only a dangerous element in "human nature."

Certainly in the underdeveloped world the bond of peoplehood provides an indispensable agency for the mobilization of energies needed to break decisively with the past and to muster the sacrifices needed for the future. And in the developed world, as well, related considerations apply. For when we turn to our own plight, we also face a need to identify with a special group—not one outside our borders, but beyond our reach in time—namely, the generations of the future. A crucial problem for the world of the future will be a concern for generations to come. Where will such a concern arise? Economists speak of the phenomenon of "time discount" as describing the inverted telescope through which humanity looks to the future, estimating the present worth of objects to be enjoyed in the future far below their worth if they could be instantly transferred to the present. This consequent devaluation of the future is generally considered to be an entirely *rational* response to the uncertainties of life. But if we apply this same calculus of "reason" to the human prospect, we face the horrendous possibility that humanity may react to the approach of environmental danger by indulging in a vast fling while it is still possible—a fling entirely justified by the estimation of present enjoyments over future ones. On what private, "rational" considerations, after all, should we make sacrifices now to ease the lot of generations whom we will never live to see?

There is only one possible answer to this question. It lies in our capacity to form a collective bond of identity with those future generations.

Contemporary industrial man, his appetite for the present whetted by the values of a high-consumption society and his attitude toward the future influenced by the prevailing canons of self-concern, has but a limited motivation to form such bonds. There are many who would sacrifice much for their children; fewer who would do so for their grandchildren. *Indeed, it is the absence of just such a bond with the future that casts doubt on the ability of nation-states or socio-economic orders to take now the measures needed to mitigate the problems of the future.*

Is it possible that in another kind of society—one in which it is no longer permissible to indulge in high consumption, perhaps no longer in vogue to set such store by the calculus of selfishness parading as reason —such an identificatory sense could be strengthened? We do not know. Nor do we know to what degree the freedoms and delights of individual self-expression

115

could survive the pressures that would intensify upon the individual in such a community Yet, if the stakes are not those of pleasure but of survival, if the absolute top priority becomes the matter of self-preservation rather than the preservation of the more agreeable aspects of our self-indulgent culture, then I am inclined to believe that the saving element in "human nature" is likely to be that very capability for identification which, in its present political manifestations, also poses some of the most dangerous challenges for the immediate future.

I am quite certain that we have not begun to exhaust the generalizations that can be risked with regard to the political forces at work in history, and I must stress as strongly as possible that I do not have in mind the formulation of an all-embracing "theory" of political behavior. I have entirely omitted for example, the crucial problem of aggression, individual or national, first examined by Freud and since elaborated by many others. I have left unexplored the work of Max Weber or Michels and their followers on the political dynamics of bureaucracy. I have done so in part because the two attributes of "human nature" that I have singled out seem to me to have been neglected, and still more because these attributes seem especially relevant, in a positive sense, to the long-term prospect for survival.

Admittedly, the capacities for submission to power and for identification lack the sense of a clear-cut "dynamics" that is the special characteristic of socio-economic behavior. Yet in calling our attention to the presence of primal elements in the shaping forces of the political future they serve the useful purpose of tempering our expectations with regard to the capacity of socio-economic orders, as such, to cope with the future. That capacity must reckon with the need for—perhaps the ultimate reliance on—welcomed hierarchies of power and strongly felt bonds of peoplehood, to the discomfiture of those who would hope that the challenges of the human prospect would finally banish the thralldoms of authority and ideology and foster the "liberation" of the individual. Our analysis provides a warning that these hopes are not likely to be realized, and that the tensions immanent in socio-economic trends must be worked out within and through the political elements in "human nature." Thus our analysis gives substance to some of the "conservative" reservations with respect to historical change that we find in classical political philosophy, and thereby constitutes a sobering counterbalance to the "radical" expectations that are founded to a large extent on the dynamics of socio-economic change.

The point is important enough to warrant some further elaboration. An essential difficulty in our estimate of the human prospect is the apparent conflict between our intuitive sense of the fixity of "human nature" and our knowledge that behavior can be altered. According to one of the radical tenets, "man makes himself," and is therefore capable of far-reaching changes in his "nature." The conservative takes a more pessimistic view, stressing the presence of a core of "human nature" that offers limits to the possibilities for change. I have sought to avoid the rather vague, and often theological, foreboding that equates this core with "evil," and to suggest that it is better regarded as the psychological substratum of the human personality whose presence we have come to recognize in many areas of behavior and should therefore acknowledge in the sphere of political attitudes as well.

From another view, moreover, I am not so sure that the conservative view is tantamount to a pessimistic view. "Pessimism about man serves to maintain the status quo," writes Leon Eisenberg.[3] Our speculations enlighten us with regard to certain aspects of the "status quo" in *all* societies, such as the susceptibility of men to the submissive requirements of political power and to the fantasies of national "identity" or "purpose," but they do not in themselves offer justification for any particular institutions such as private property, nor do they serve as rationales for the immoral use of political power.

A conservative view of the political element in society must not, therefore, be interpreted as attempt-

3. Leon Eisenberg, "The *Human* Nature of Human Nature," *Science*, April 14, 1972, p. 124.

ing to fix humanity in a vise. Any claim that the quality of social existence is inexorably determined by the "nature" of man is refuted out of hand by the most cursory examination of the range of morality and human sensibility to be found in the various nations of the world. There remains, nonetheless, the contention that this plasticity of culture must accommodate itself in some manner or other to the needs that spring from man's infant and childhood conditioning, and this does not permit us to assume that the political structure of society can accommodate itself to whatever image we may have of what man should be.

This last consideration is of the essence. The assumption that man ultimately "makes himself" in a benign manner implies that within the raw stuff of the human infant there exists some gyroscopic tendency that will finally guide him, as an adult, in a direction that will accord with the radical's high moral estimate of mankind. Otherwise, why should we not conclude that the self-made man, stripped of all his false consciousness, divested of the delusions and fantasies that have misled him, will settle into a state of utter existential despair, or relapse into a suicidal solipsism? Indeed, why not conclude that before the terrifying truth of mortal finitude each man must shed the frail moral teachings of the past and finish his life in an orgy of self-indulgence that knows no bounds? As we have suggested, that truly pessimistic possibility must look for its refutation to the persistent promptings of a

119

portion of man's being that he does not "make," but
that makes him. In this regard it is worth reflecting that
the hideous visions of man's future in Huxley's *Brave
New World,* or Orwell's *1984* are both based on the
premise of the unlimited plasticity and malleability of
the human species.

It is possible, of course, that in the future men
may be so altered in their genetic characters, or
nurtured in such carefully planned circumstances, that
the "class" or "patriotic" attributes of political life
would disappear because they no longer answered to
an inner need. But at this juncture in history, our
attention had better be focused on what men are likely
to be, rather than on what they could eventually
become. The human prospect forces us to deal with
human change within an indeterminate, but not indefinite, time period, and speculations as to the degree of
potential change must give way before the degree of
change that is imaginable within that period.

So far as the genetic question is concerned, the
time required for change is very long indeed, unless
we discover chemical means of altering human behavior and apply these on a global scale—a prospect still
happily well beyond reach. Writing in a symposium on
behavior, E. O. Wilson presents the following "optimistic" estimate:

[T]here is every justification from both genetic theory
and experiments on animal species to suppose that rapid
behavioral evolution is at least a possibility in man. By rapid

I mean significant alteration in, say, emotional and intellectual traits within no more than ten generations—or about 300 years. [4]

Unfortunately, three hundred years, however rapid in the eye of the anthropologist, is hopelessly slow for the challenges now gathering on the horizon. Moreover, Wilson does not specify the changes in social institutions that might be required to bring about the accelerated evolution in the direction of social improvement.

As for the rapidity with which these institutional changes can work their effect on behavior, we face the problem of the natural "inertia" of the human condition, an inertia ascribable not only to the presence of a stubbornly persisting substratum of psychological needs but also to the laggard pace of change in the family setting through which those needs are gradually shaped into the attitudes of adult behavior. In his sympathetic but critical summary of Marx's view of man, Bertell Ollman vividly describes this process:

People acquire most of their personal and class characteristics in childhood. It is the conditions operating then, transmitted primarily by the family, which makes them what they are, at least as regards basic responses; and, in most cases, what they are will vary very little over their lives. Thus, even where the conditions people have been brought up in change by the time they reach maturity, their

4. E. O. Wilson, "Competitive and Aggressive Behavior," in *Man and Beast* (Smithsonian Institution, 1971), p. 207.

characters still reflect the situation which has passed on. If Marx had studied the family more closely, surely he would have noticed that as a factory for producing character it is invariably a generation or more behind the times, producing people who, tomorrow, will be able to deal with yesterday's problems.[5]

I do not raise these considerations to dismiss the possibility of dramatic transformations in social organization, such as we have seen in China. Indeed, I am persuaded that changes of at least this degree of penetration and revolutionary impact will be required within the time span with which our examination has been concerned. My analysis leads me, rather, to reiterate that these behavioral alterations, much as those in China, will have to allow for, or build on, recalcitrant elements in the human personality, including the two that I have singled out for emphasis, namely, the "hunger" for political authority and the "fantasy" of political identification. Further, it is not genetic evolution or cumulative amelioration in rearing that is likely to be the crucial implementing factor in affecting the behavioral reorientations of the "post-industrial" future, but the use of those primal elements on which political power rests—a belief for which, once again, the Chinese experience provides supporting evidence.

I am all too aware that these conclusions may bring dismay to many whom I consider my friends and

5. Bertell Ollman, *Alienation: Marx's Conception of Man in Capitalist Society* (Cambridge University Press, 1971), p. 241.

comfort to many whom I consider my foes. To suggest that political power and hierarchy serve a supportive function in society plays directly into the hands of those who applaud the "orderliness" of authoritarian or dictatorial governments. To find a reason for the appeal of nonrational political beliefs is to encourage those who advocate irresponsible political programs. To stress the psychological roots of peoplehood is to weaken the cause of whose who seek to overcome the curse of racism and xenophobia.

If I nonetheless publish these thoughts, with all their potential mischievousness, it is for two reasons. The first is that the weakest part of the humanitarian outlook, both philosophically and pragmatically, has been its inability or unwillingness to come to grips with certain obdurate human characteristics. As a result we find buried within "humanist" appeals a conception of human nature that is often as reactionary, in the sense of ascribing an inherent element of evil to man, as that of the most unthinking conservative. Let me cite this example from a contemporary radical publication:

> In the most profound sense, the proletariat has not one enemy but two—the ruling class and itself. In the absence of a humanizing militancy and a militant humanism, in the absence of a fierce common hatred for the common enemy, and a fiercer common love for the proletariat as a whole, history will degenerate into barbarism.[6]

6. "The Making of Socialist Consciousness," by the editors of *Socialist Revolution* (1970), reprinted in *The Capitalist System*, eds. R.C. Edwards, Reich, and Weiskopf (Prentice-Hall, 1972), p. 505.

Extended commentary hardly seems necessary. The encouragement of aggressive impulses (militancy, fierce hatred, fiercer love), the dehumanization implicit in the admonition to "love" the proletariat "as a whole", and above all the view of man as engaged in a struggle to the death with himself, open this view to a critique as scathing as any that could be directed against a "bourgeois" conception of humanity. If radicalism is to go to the roots, as the term implies, it must be prepared to examine the "nature" of man in ways much more courageous and much less pietistic than those it uses in the name of "humanism." Only on such a basis can it hope to build ideas and programs that may be able to withstand the tempest of events whose source lies, both as challenge and response, within men themselves.

My second reason for advancing these views relates to the first. I have tried to take the measure of man as a creature of his socio-economic arrangements and his political bonds. It may be that from some other perspective the prospect for collective human adaptation would seem brighter. But from the vantage point of this book, a failure to recognize the limitations and difficulties of our capacities for response would only build an architecture of hope on false beliefs.

FIVE

Final Reflections on the Human Prospect

WHAT IS NEEDED NOW is a summing up of the human prospect, some last reflections on its implications for the present and future alike.

The external challenges can be succinctly reviewed. We are entering a period in which rapid population growth, the presence of obliterative weapons, and dwindling resources will bring international tensions to dangerous levels for an extended period. Indeed, there seems no reason for these levels of danger to subside unless population equilibrium is achieved and some rough measure of equity reached in the distribution of wealth among nations, either by great increases in the output of the underdeveloped world or by a massive redistribution of wealth from the richer to the poorer lands.

Whether such an equitable arrangement can be reached—at least within the next several generations—is open to serious doubt. Transfers of adequate magnitude imply a willingness to redistribute income internationally on a more generous scale than the advanced nations have evidenced within their own

127

domains. The required increases in output in the backward regions would necessitate gargantuan applications of energy merely to extract the needed resources. It is uncertain whether the requisite energy-producing technology exists, and, more serious, possible that its application would bring us to the threshold of an irreversible change in climate as a consequence of the enormous addition of man-made heat to the atmosphere.

It is this last problem that poses the most demanding and difficult of the challenges. The existing pace of industrial growth, with no allowance for increased industrialization to repair global poverty, holds out the risk of entering the danger zone of climatic change in as little as three or four generations. If that trajectory is in fact pursued, industrial growth will then have to come to an immediate halt, for another generation or two along that path would literally consume human, perhaps all, life. That terrifying outcome can be postponed only to the extent that the wastage of heat can be reduced, or that technologies that do not add to the atmospheric heat burden—for example, the use of solar energy—can be utilized. The outlook can also be mitigated by redirecting output away from heat-creating material outputs into the production of "services" that add only trivially to heat.

All these considerations make the designation of a timetable for industrial deceleration difficult to construct. Yet, under any and all assumptions, one irrefutable conclusion remains. The industrial growth process, so central to the economic and social life of capitalism and Western socialism alike, will be forced to slow down, in all likelihood within a generation or two, and will probably have to give way to decline thereafter. To repeat the words of the text, "whether we are unable to sustain growth or unable to tolerate it," the long era of industrial expansion is now entering its final stages, and we must anticipate the commencement of a new era of stationary total output and (if population growth continues or an equitable sharing among nations has not yet been attained) declining material output per head in the advanced nations.

These challenges also point to a certain time frame within which different aspects of the human prospect will assume different levels of importance. In the short run, by which we may speak of the decade immediately ahead, no doubt the most pressing questions will be those of the use and abuse of national power, the vicissitudes of the narrative of political history, perhaps the short-run vagaries of the economic process, about which we have virtually no predictive capability whatsoever. From our vantage point today, another crisis in the Middle East, further Vietnams or Czechoslovakias, inflation, severe economic malfunction—or their avoidance—are sure to exercise the primary influence over the quality of existence, or even over the possibilities for existence.

In a somewhat longer time frame—extending perhaps for a period of a half century—the main shaping force of the future takes on a different aspect. Assuming that the day-to-day, year-to-year crises are surmounted in relative safety, the issue of the relative resilience and adaptive capabilities of the two great socio-economic systems comes to the fore as the decisive question. Here the properties of industrial socialism and capitalism as ideal types seem likely to provide the parameters within which and by which the prospect for man will be formed. We have already indicated what general tendencies seem characteristic of each of these systems, and the advantages that may accrue to socialist—that is, planned and probably authoritarian social orders—during this era of adjustment.

In the long run, stretching a century or more ahead, still a different facet of the human prospect appears critical. This is the transformational problem, centered in the reconstruction of the material basis of civilization itself. In this period, as indefinite in its boundaries but as unmistakable in its mighty dimensions as a vast storm visible on the horizon, the challenge devolves upon those deep-lying capabilities for political change whose roots in "human nature" have been the subject of our last chapter.

It is the challenges of the middle and the long run that command our attention when we speculate about the human prospect, if only because those of the short run defy our prognostic grasp entirely. It seems

130

unnecessary to add more than a word to underline the magnitude of these still distant problems. No developing country has fully confronted the implications of becoming a "modern" nation-state whose industrial development must be severely limited, or considered the strategy for such a state in a world in which the Western nations, capitalist and socialist both, will continue for a long period to enjoy the material advantages of their early start. Within the advanced nations, in turn, the difficulties of adjustment are no less severe. No capitalist nation has as yet imagined the extent of the alterations it must undergo to attain a viable stationary socio-economic structure, and no socialist state has evidenced the needed willingness to subordinate its national interests to supra-national ones.

To these obstacles we must add certain elements of the political propensities in "human nature" that stand in the way of a rational, orderly adaptation of the industrial mode in the directions that will become increasingly urgent as the distant future comes closer. There seems no hope for rapid changes in the human character traits that would have to be modified to bring about a peaceful, organized reorientation of life styles. Men and women, much as they are today, will set the pace and determine the necessary means for the social changes that will eventually have to be made. The drift toward the strong exercise of political power—a movement given its initial momentum by the need to exercise a much wider and deeper administration of both production and consumption—is likely to attain added support from the psychological insecurity that will be sharpened in a period of unrest and uncertainty. The bonds of national identity are certain to exert their powerful force, mobilizing men for the collective efforts needed but inhibiting the international sharing of burdens and wealth. The myopia that confines the present vision of men to the short-term future is not likely to disappear overnight, rendering still more difficult a planned and orderly retrenchment and redivision of output.

Therefore the outlook is for what we may call "convulsive change"—change forced upon us by external events rather than by conscious choice, by catastrophe rather than by calculation. As with Malthus's much derided but all too prescient forecasts, nature will provide the checks, if foresight and "morality" do not. One such check could be the outbreak of wars arising from the explosive tensions of the coming period, which might reduce the growth rates of the surviving nation-states and thereby defer the danger of industrial asphyxiation for a period. Alternatively, nature may rescue us from ourselves by what John Platt has called a "storm of crisis problems."[1] As we breach now this, now that edge of environmental tolerance, local disasters—large-scale fatal urban tempera-

1. John Platt, "What We Must Do," *Science*, Nov.28,1969, p.1115.

ture inversions, massive crop failures, resource shortages—may also slow down economic growth and give
a necessary impetus to the piecemeal construction of
an ecologically and socially viable social system.

Such negative feedbacks are likely to exercise an
all-important dampening effect on a crisis that would
otherwise in all probability overwhelm the slender human capabilities for planned adjustment to the future.
However brutal these feedbacks, they are apt to prove
effective in changing our attitudes as well as our
actions, unlike appeals to our collective foresight,
such as the exhortations of the Club of Rome's *Limits
to Growth,* or the manifesto of a group of British
scientists calling for an immediate halt to growth.[2]
The problem is that the challenge to survival still lies
sufficiently far in the future, and the inertial momentum of the present industrial order is still so great, that
no substantial voluntary diminution of growth, much
less a planned reorganization of society, is today even
remotely imaginable. What leader of an underdeveloped nation, particularly one caught up in the
exhilaration of a revolutionary restructuring of society, would call a halt to industrial activity in his
impoverished land? What capitalist or socialist nation
would put a ceiling on material output, limiting its
citizens to the well-being obtainable from its present
volume of production?

Thus, however admirable in intent, impassioned

2. "Blueprint for Survival," *The Ecologist,* Jan. 1972.

polemics against growth are exercises in futility today. Worse, they may even point in the wrong direction. Paradoxically, perhaps, the priorities for the present lie in the temporary encouragement of the very process of industrial advance that is ultimately the mortal enemy. In the backward areas, the acute misery that is the potential source of so much international disruption can be remedied only to the extent that rapid improvements are introduced, including that minimal infrastructure needed to support a modern system of health services, education, transportation, fertilizer production, and the like. In the developed nations, what is required at the moment is the encouragement of technical advances that will permit the extraction of new resources to replace depleted reserves of scarce minerals, new sources of energy to stave off the collapse that would occur if present energy reservoirs were exhausted before substitutes were discovered, and, above all, new techniques for the generation of energy that will minimize the associated generation of heat.

Thus there is a short period left during which we can safely continue on the present trajectory. It is possible that during this period a new direction will be struck that will greatly ease the otherwise inescapable adjustments. The underdeveloped nations, making a virtue of necessity, may redefine "development" in ways that minimize the need for the accumulation of capital, stressing instead the education and vitality of their citizens. The possibilities of such an historic step would be much enhanced were the advanced nations to lead the way by a major effort to curtail the enormous wastefulness of industrial production as it is used today. If these changes took place, we might even look forward to a still more desirable redirection of history in a diminution of scale, a reduction in the size of the human community from the dangerous level of immense nation-states toward the "polis" that defined the appropriate reach of political power for the ancient Greeks.

All these are possibilities, but certainly not probabilities. The revitalization of the polis is hardly likely to take place during a period in which an orderly response to social and physical challenges will require an increase of centralized power and the encouragement of national rather than communal attitudes. The voluntary abandonment of the industrial mode of production would require a degree of self-abnegation on the part of its beneficiaries—managers and consumers alike—that would be without parallel in history. The redefinition of development on the part of the poorer nations would require a prodigious effort of will in the face of the envy and fear that Western industrial power and "affluence" will arouse.

Thus in all likelihood we must brace ourselves for the consequences of which we have spoken—the risk of "wars of redistribution" or of "preemptive seizure," the rise of social tensions in the industrialized

135

nations over the division of an ever more slow-growing or even diminishing product, and the prospect of a
far more coercive exercise of national power as the
means by which we will attempt to bring these disruptive processes under control.

From that period of harsh adjustment, I can see
no realistic escape. Rationalize as we will, stretch the
figures as favorably as honesty will permit, we cannot
reconcile the requirements for a lengthy continuation
of the present rate of industrialization of the globe
with the capacity of existing resources or the fragile
biosphere to permit or to tolerate the effects of that
industrialization. Nor is it easy to foresee a willing
acquiescence of humankind, individually or through
its existing social organizations, in the alterations of
lifeways that foresight would dictate. If then, by the
question "Is there hope for man?" we ask whether it
is possible to meet the challenges of the future without
the payment of a fearful price, the answer must be:
No, there is no such hope.

At this final stage of our inquiry, with the full
spectacle of the human prospect before us, the spirit
quails and the will falters. We find ourselves pressed
to the very limit of our personal capacities, not alone
in summoning up the courage to look squarely at the
dimensions of the impending predicament, but in
finding words that can offer some plausible relief in a
situation so bleak. There is now nowhere to turn other

than to those private beliefs and disbeliefs that guide each of us through life, and whose disconcerting presence was the first problem with which we had to deal in appraising the prospect before us. I shall therefore speak my mind without any pretense that the words I am about to write have any basis other than those subjective promptings from which I was forced to begin and in which I must now discover whatever consolation I can offer after the analysis to which they have driven me.

At this late juncture I have no intention of sounding a call for moral awakening or for social action on some unrealistic scale. Yet, I do not intend to condone, much less to urge, an attitude of passive resignation, or a relegation of the human prospect to the realm of things we choose not to think about. Avoidable evil remains, as it always will, an enemy that can be defeated; and the fact that the collective destiny of man portends unavoidable travail is no reason, and cannot be tolerated as an excuse, for doing nothing. This general admonition applies in particular to the intellectual elements of Western nations whose privileged role as sentries for society takes on a special importance in the face of things as we now see them. It is their task not only to prepare their fellow citizens for the sacrifices that will be required of them but to take the lead in seeking to redefine the legitimate boundaries of power and the permissible sanctuaries of freedom, for a future in which the exercise of power

137

must inevitably increase and many present areas of freedom, especially in economic life, be curtailed.

Let me therefore put these last words in a somewhat more "positive" frame, offsetting to some degree the bleakness of our prospect, without violating the facts or spirit of our inquiry. Here I must begin by stressing for one last time an essential fact. The human prospect is not an irrevocable death sentence. It is not an inevitable doomsday toward which we are headed, although the risk of enormous catastrophes exists. The prospect is better viewed as a formidable array of challenges that must be overcome before human survival is assured, before we can move *beyond doomsday.* These challenges can be overcome—by the saving intervention of nature if not by the wisdom and foresight of man. The death sentence is therefore better viewed as a contingent life sentence—one that will permit the continuance of human society, but only on a basis very different from that of the present, and probably only after much suffering during the period of transition.

What sort of society might eventually emerge? As I have said more than once, I believe the long-term solution requires nothing less than the gradual abandonment of the lethal techniques, the uncongenial lifeways, and the dangerous mentality of industrial civilization itself. The dimensions of such a transformation into a "post-industrial" society have already been touched upon, and cannot be greatly elaborated here:

in all probability the extent and ramifications of change are as unforeseeable from our contemporary vantage point as present-day society would have been unimaginable to a speculative observer a thousand years ago.

Yet I think a few elements of the society of the post-industrial era can be discerned. Although we cannot know on what technical foundation it will rest, we can be certain that many of the accompaniments of an industrial order must be absent. To repeat once again what we have already said, the societal view of production and consumption must stress parsimonious, not prodigal, attitudes. Resource-consuming and heat-generating processes must be regarded as necessary evils, not as social triumphs, to be relegated to as small a portion of economic life as possible. This implies a sweeping reorganization of the mode of production in ways that cannot be foretold, but that would seem to imply the end of the giant factory, the huge office, perhaps of the urban complex.

What values and ways of thought would be congenial to such a radical reordering of things we also cannot know, but it is likely that the ethos of "science," so intimately linked with industrial application, would play a much reduced role. In the same way, it seems probable that a true post-industrial society would witness the waning of the work ethic that is also intimately entwined with our industrial society. As one critic has pointed out, even Marx,

despite his bitter denunciation of the alienating effects
of labor in a capitalist milieu, placed his faith in the
presumed "liberating" effects of labor in a socialist
society, and did not consider a "terrible secret"—that
even the most creative work may be only "a neurotic
activity that diverts the mind from the diminution of
time and the approach of death."[3]

It is therefore possible that a post-industrial society would also turn in the direction of many pre-industrial societies—toward the exploration of inner states
of experience rather than the outer world of fact and
material accomplishment. Tradition and ritual, the pil-
lars of life in virtually all societies other than those of
an industrial character, would probably once again
assert their ancient claims as the guide to and solace
for life. The struggle for individual achievement, especially for material ends, is likely to give way to the
acceptance of communally organized and ordained
roles.

This is by no means an effort to portray a future
utopia. On the contrary, many of these possible attributes of a post-industrial society are deeply repugnant
to my twentieth-century temper as well as incompati-
ble with my most treasured privileges. The search for
scientific knowledge, the delight in intellectual heresy,
the freedom to order one's life as one pleases, are not
likely to be easily contained within the tradition-

3. John Diggins, "Thoreau, Marx, and the Riddle of Alienation,"
Social Research, Winter 1973, p. 573.

oriented, static society I have depicted. To a very great degree, the public must take precedence over the private—an aim to which it is easy to give lip service in the abstract but difficult for someone used to the pleasures of political, social, and intellectual freedom to accept in fact.

These are all necessarily prophetic speculations, offered more in the spirit of providing some vision of the future, however misty, than as a set of predictions to be "rigorously" examined. In these half-blind gropings there is, however, one element in which we can place credence, although it offers uncertainty as well as hope. This is our knowledge that some human societies have existed for millennia, and that others can probably exist for future millennia, in a continuous rhythm of birth and coming of age and death, without pressing toward those dangerous ecological limits, or engendering those dangerous social tensions, that threaten present-day "advanced" societies. In our discovery of "primitive" cultures, living out their timeless histories, we may have found the single most important object lesson for future man.

What we do not know, but can only hope, is that future man can rediscover the self-renewing vitality of primitive culture without reverting to its levels of ignorance and cruel anxiety. It may be the sad lesson of the future that no civilization is without its pervasive "malaise," each expressing in its own way the ineradicable fears of the only animal that contemplates its own death, but at least the human activities expressing that malaise need not, as is the case in our time, threaten the continuance of life itself.

All this goes, perhaps, beyond speculation to fantasy. But something more substantial than speculation or fantasy is needed to sustain men through the long trials ahead. For the driving energy of modern man has come from his Promethean spirit, his nervous will, his intellectual daring. It is this spirit that has enabled him to work miracles, above all to subjugate nature to his will, and to create societies designed to free man from his animal bondage.

Some of that Promethean spirit may still serve us in good stead in the years of transition. But it is not a spirit that conforms easily with the shape of future society as I have imagined it; worse, within that impatient spirit lurks one final danger for the years during which we must watch the approach of an unwanted future. This is the danger that can be glimpsed in our deep consciousness when we take stock of things as they now are: the wish that the drama run its full tragic course, bringing man, like a Greek hero, to the fearful end that he has, however unwittingly, arranged for himself. For it is not only with dismay that Promethean man regards the future. It is also with a kind of anger. If after so much effort, so little has been accomplished; if before such vast challenges, so little is apt to be done—then let the drama proceed to its finale, let mankind suffer the end it deserves.

Such a view is by no means the expression of only a few perverse minds. On the contrary, it is the application to the future of the prevailing attitudes with which our age regards the present. When men can generally acquiesce in, even relish, the destruction of their living contemporaries, when they can regard with indifference or irritation the fate of those who live in slums, rot in prison, or starve in lands that have meaning only insofar as they are vacation resorts, why should they be expected to take the painful actions needed to prevent the destruction of future generations whose faces they will never live to see? Worse yet, will they not curse these future generations whose claims to life can be honored only by sacrificing present enjoyments; and will they not, if it comes to a choice, condemn them to nonexistence by choosing the present over the future?

The question, then, is how we are to summon up the will to survive—not perhaps in the distant future, where survival will call on those deep sources of imagined human unity, but in the present and near-term future, while we still enjoy and struggle with the heritage of our personal liberties, our atomistic existences.

At this last moment of reflection another figure from Greek mythology comes to mind. It is that of Atlas, bearing with endless perseverance the weight of the heavens in his hands. If mankind is to rescue life, it must first preserve the very will to live, and thereby rescue the future from the angry condemnation of the present. The spirit of conquest and aspiration will not provide the inspiration it needs for this task. It is the example of Atlas, resolutely bearing his burden, that provides the strength we seek. If, within us, the spirit of Atlas falters, there perishes the determination to preserve humanity at all cost and any cost, forever.

But Atlas is, of course, no other but ourselves. Myths have their magic power because they cast on the screen of our imaginations, like the figures of the heavenly constellations, immense projections of our own hopes and capabilities. We do not know with certainty that humanity will survive, but it is a comfort to know that there exist within us the elements of fortitude and will from which the image of Atlas springs.

ACKNOWLEDGMENTS /
INDEX

Acknowledgments

I AM INDEBTED TO many people for their help in writing this book—some for technical advice, some for detailed criticism, some simply for their counsel and encouragement. I will not embarrass my friends and colleagues by revealing the extent of their complicity in this book. Let me therefore list them alphabetically: Moses Abramovitz, Daniel Bell, Stanley Burnshaw, Paul Ehrlich, John Holdren, Arien and Irving Howe, Robert Silvers, Hans Staudinger, Thomas Vietorisz. One name only I place out of order because I know that its bearer is willing to be excused from the usual disclaimer that frees all the above from any responsibility for the content of these pages. As always, I salute Adolph Lowe, the spiritual co-author of these pages and the original source of the metaphor of Atlas.[1] Finally, let me thank my secretary, Ms. Salzman. I do not think there is a Perfect Secretary in

1. See "S ist noch nicht P," in *Ernst Bloch zu ehren* (Frankfurt am Main, 1965), p. 142. Professor Daniel Bell has pointed out that Bertrand Russell (unbeknownst to Professor Lowe or myself) used the metaphor of "a weary but unyielding Atlas" in a moving conclusion to his essay "A Free Man's Worship" (1903).

147

the Greek gallery of the gods, but if there were, her name would surely be Lillian.

A brief word on sources. I have sought to identify all quotations and to underpin with citations those parts of the argument in which scientific expertise is critical. I have not burdened the text with appeals to authority for the economic, sociological, or psychoanalytic sections of the text, save in occasional places where a reader might wish to know of a parallel argument. So much of the book is built on the foundation of my life as well as my studies that extensive footnoting seemed pointless: unnecessary to those who will accept the message of the book as it now stands, unavailing to those who will not.

Index

Index